DOUBLEDAY
CELEBRATES
100 YEARS OF
EXCELLENCE

WHO ARE THE PROMISE KEEPERS?

Understanding the Christian Men's Movement

KEN ABRAHAM

DOUBLEDAY
New York   London   Toronto   Sydney   Auckland

PUBLISHED BY DOUBLEDAY
a division of Bantam Doubleday Dell Publishing Group, Inc.
1540 Broadway, New York, New York 10036

DOUBLEDAY and the portrayal of an anchor with a dolphin are
trademarks of Doubleday, a division of Bantam Doubleday Dell
Publishing Group, Inc.

Names of some individuals have been changed to protect their privacy.
Some stories represent composites.

The Power of a Promise Kept, edited by Gregg Lewis and published by
Focus on the Family. Copyright © 1995, Promise Keepers. All rights
reserved. International copyright secured. Used by permission.

Seven Promises of a Promise Keeper, edited and published by Focus on
the Family. Copyright © 1994, Promise Keepers. All rights reserved.
International copyright secured. Used by permission.

Book Design by Stanley S. Drate/Folio Graphics Co., Inc.

Library of Congress Cataloging-in-Publication Data

Abraham, Ken.
    Who are the Promise Keepers? : understanding the Christian men's
movement / Ken Abraham. — 1st ed.
        p.   cm.
    Includes bibliographical references.
    1. Promise Keepers (Organization)   I. Title.
    BV960.A27   1997
    267'.23—dc21   97-1777
                                                                  CIP

ISBN 0-385-48699-5

To my mother and father, Minnie and Howard Abraham, who taught me the value of keeping promises long before I ever heard of Promise Keepers.

And to my wife, Angela Abraham, and my children, Ashleigh and Alyssa: May I be as true to my word to you as my parents have been to me.

ACKNOWLEDGMENTS

Nobody authors a book alone nowadays. Most modern books are a group effort, with the author being only one of many people who work together to make the final product something that the public will want to read. This book is no exception. I am extremely grateful to my friend Greg Johnson for believing in me, and to Mark Fretz, of Doubleday, for believing enough in Greg to take him at his word.

I am also deeply indebted to my friend Lonnie Hull DuPont for reading the manuscript and making numerous suggestions, especially in regard to how women view Promise Keepers. Lonnie, if the dog or cat ever bear offspring, I'm sending them to you!

Tim Jones did a masterful job in editing the manuscript, helping me to maintain my objectivity in a project that continually begged me to take sides. Elizabeth Walter kept us all on the same page. Thanks, Elizabeth!

Bob and Kathy Blume, super-facilitators—without you, this book would have been much more difficult to write and far less enjoyable. You two are the best!

Thanks, too, to Bob (Roady Ralph) Hegedus, Jan Kozik, Melissa and Jerry Kovach, and Michael Briggs for helping me research this project. Special thanks to the photographers, Thom Hickling, Brent Pirie, and Norman Seow, whose photos appear within these pages, and to my brother, Tink, for coordinating them.

To Jim Walthour, my friend, mentor, and fellow golf duffer, who took that first book to the publisher so many years ago—with every page I write, may you know that you have played a key part.

And a special thanks to the outstanding sales and marketing staff at Doubleday. Thank you for all your hard work in opening doors so that the world may know.

—KEN ABRAHAM

CONTENTS

1 "WHERE'S THE BEER?"   *1*

2 A COACH'S DREAM   *16*

3 PROMISES, PROMISES   *32*

4 PROMISES TO EACH OTHER   *45*

5 TAKING IT TO THE STREETS   *65*

6 THE KEEPERS OF THE PROMISES   *82*

7 PROMISE KEEPERS AND WOMEN   *99*

8 ARE PROMISE KEEPERS RACISTS?   *123*

9 CHRISTIANS OPPOSED TO PROMISE KEEPERS   *143*

10 PROMISE KEEPERS AND REPUBLICANS   *159*

11 PROMISE KEEPERS AND THE WORLD   *171*

12 PROMISE KEEPERS AND YOU   *181*

NOTES   *205*

WHO ARE THE PROMISE KEEPERS?

CHAPTER 1

"WHERE'S THE BEER?"

"Hey, where's the beer?" bellowed Barry, a balding fellow in his early forties whose belly confirmed his obvious taste for the brew. As Barry and his buddies piled out of a van in the parking lot of Three Rivers Stadium in Pittsburgh, he turned to one of the men and asked, "How are we supposed to have a tailgate party with no beer?"

"No beer this weekend, Barry," answered Tom, a ruggedly handsome, sandy-haired guy in his mid-thirties. "We won't be having a tailgate party. Besides," Tom added as he slapped Barry on his broad back, "we don't need any beer to get rowdy this weekend. We're going to have something better than beer. This is Promise Keepers." Tom and his buddies started across the parking lot toward Gate C of the stadium, leaving Barry standing hesitantly on the pavement.

Finally, Barry called, "Wait for me!" and hurried to catch up to the others. As he passed me, I heard him mutter, "Something better than beer? What did I get myself into?"

1

What indeed? Just what is the phenomenon known as Promise Keepers?

I had been following the Promise Keepers movement for several years, tracking it in the news and interviewing numerous people involved in various levels of the organization. I had read everything I could get my hands on about the group that David Blankenhorn, author of the bestselling *Fatherless America*, referred to as "the largest and most important men's movement in the United States today."[1]

Several of my friends had attended Promise Keepers conferences over the past three years. Invariably, they came away raving about the experience they had had in a stadium packed with men—only men—singing ditties about God and listening to fifteen hours of lectures, all while sitting on hard stadium seats. Why would I want to attend something like that? I had heard men singing out of key before, and I had endured enough lectures, sermons, and motivational talks in my life to leave me with no interest in attending a mental marathon.

Yet I could not shake the notion that something significant was happening through the Promise Keepers conferences, judging from the apparent changes in the lives of the men who attended them. I had, after all, witnessed the late-1980s men's movement spawned by Robert Bly's bestselling book *Iron John*, which, for a while, had made it fashionable for fellows to gather in the woods all weekend to howl like wolves and beat their bare chests like tom-toms in an effort to connect with the supposed "wild man" within. Sam Keen's book *Fire in the Belly* followed in 1991 and gave the early '90s men's movement a New Age twist, encouraging men to embark upon a new "hero's journey," moving from brokenness to wholeness in every area of their lives . . . whatever that meant. Both Bly's wild men and Keen's heroes gave up the quest rather quickly, neither group sustaining a prolonged impact. The much ballyhooed men's movement stalled in its tracks, as stymied men grew impatient trying to find the true meaning of their maleness within themselves.

On the other hand, Promise Keepers, which encourages men to look beyond themselves to God in search of meaning, has continued to explode since its first major conference, increasing from a "mere" 4,200 men in 1993 to more than one million men in 1996—and it's still growing. If for no other reason than the enormous number of men affected by this movement, I felt compelled to attend a conference and check it out for myself.

I approached my first "live" Promise Keepers experience with as few preconceived conclusions as possible. I felt that any movement that encouraged men to be better husbands, fathers, and citizens could not be all bad. On the other hand, the skeptic in me had difficulty believing that Promise Keepers could possibly be as good as my friends had described it.

I had heard the sarcastic remarks of media pundits, of course, poking fun at Promise Keepers' rah-rah, "Let's go win one for God!" spirit. I was also well aware of the vocal criticism by women's groups that Promise Keepers encourages men to oppress women. They complain that Promise Keepers is a "guy thing" and that females are purposely excluded. Some radical feminists label Promise Keepers' emphasis upon male leadership in the home as a patriarchal, reactionary attempt by the movement to return male-female roles to those of the pre-bra-burning era of the early 1950s. They fear that the goal is to push males to new heights from which they might dominate females.

On the broader social issue of racism, Promise Keepers has been disparaged for doing too little too slowly, even if it is one of the most vocal groups addressing racial issues in our day. But for all the Promise Keepers rhetoric about racial and denominational reconciliation, the overwhelming majority of Promise Keepers are white Protestants.

Other critics worry that Promise Keepers wields considerable political clout. An article in *The Nation* warned that "Promise Keepers appears to be a new 'third wave' of the religious right, following the demise of Jerry Falwell's Moral Majority and the compromise of Pat Robertson's Christian Coalition with secular Republicanism. Yet the political significance of Promise Keepers has eluded most of the media coverage lavished upon its stadium extravaganzas, which are bedazzling and often emotionally affecting for the reporters who cover them."[2]

Because of the endorsement of evangelical Christian leaders such as Pat Robertson and "Focus on the Family" founder James Dobson—both outspoken political conservatives—many of Promise Keepers' critics accuse the movement of being a rallying point for right-leaning political agendas. Leaders within the movement adamantly deny any official political associations. Indeed, Promise Keepers as an organization is reluctant to take official positions on most political issues.

Whatever the claims of Promise Keepers' friends and foes, now, at last, I was about to find out for myself just how this movement was having such a profound impact upon so many men—and why it was generating such controversy. Barry and Tom and their friends seemed to know where they were going, so I fell in step behind.

The usual complement of stadium parking lot attendants was directing cars, vans, campers, and even a contingency of motorcyclists into the parking areas as fast as the front attendants could collect the four-dollar parking fee. I couldn't resist pausing long enough in my trek toward the stadium to ask a crusty, nearly toothless attendant, "How does the crowd coming in compare with the usual ball-game crowds?"

The attendant's demeanor changed dramatically as he stopped, thought for a moment, then replied, "This group is peaceful and polite. Never seen anything like it."

"How long have you worked here?" I asked.

"Fourteen years," he said with a saw-toothed smile, waving another car into a parking space. The driver of the car stopped to let a pickup truck cut in front of him and take the parking place the attendant had indicated. "Nope," the attendant said, shaking his head, "this isn't your ordinary bunch."

I hurried toward the stadium. It was about five o'clock on Friday afternoon; the gates had opened at 4:30 P.M. for the program scheduled to begin at 6:30 P.M. Throngs of men, many of whom wore matching bright-colored shirts or hats to identify themselves in the crowd to other members of their group, were hustling into the stadium.

Just in front of the stadium, I saw a cavernous white tent— large enough to house a football field—emblazoned with blue and white banners advertising PROMISE KEEPERS RESOURCES. I peeked around a tent flap and discovered row after row of Promise Keepers books, music tapes and CDs, T-shirts, mugs, hats, and a wide variety of other "resource material" trucked in from PK headquarters in Denver. The tent was crowded with men excitedly racing up and down the rows, poring over books and materials they would perhaps never go to a shopping mall to find, selecting their purchases and heading for the long checkout lines at each end of the tent. Oddly, at this advertised-for-men-only event, in this sea of males, the volunteer sales clerks and helpers were almost all women. I would soon discover that there were far more women working with Promise Keepers than I had ever imagined.

Many of the men in the resource tent simply browsed, perhaps stalking their prey and planning to return after the evening program. Plenty of guys, however, came out of the tent carrying armloads of materials designed to help them be better men—or at least look the part. Promise keeping has obviously become big business.

Admission to the Promise Keepers conference was not cheap—$60 in advance and $70 at the gate on the day of the event. Compared to the $45 average ticket price for a National Football League game, or the $150–$300 admission charge to a motivational seminar, I suppose Promise Keepers' pricetag for the day-and-a-half conference was reasonable. But I still had to wonder about the finances of this huge operation.

I had charged the $60 admission fee to my credit card when I had called the toll-free Promise Keepers automated registration line. Promise Keepers estimates that between February and July 1996 they received an average of twenty thousand phone calls *a day* requesting preregistration information for its various conferences. My confirmation number—or, in PK lingo, my "constituent number"—for the Pittsburgh conference held in mid-July was somewhere around 1.2 million. Even if my personal identification number was not a precise reflection of the number of 1996 attendees, which at that point had surpassed one million men, Promise Keepers was pulling in some major money. In return for my registration fee, I had received in the mail a cassette tape of Promise Keepers music, some brief instructions about what to bring to the event, and a wristband designating the city in which I would be attending a conference.

So where does the rest of the money go?

Steve Chavis, national spokesperson for Promise Keepers, later told me that 90 percent of the registration fees for each conference were spent in putting on the local event. In other words, the majority of the registration money received for the Pittsburgh conference was spent there. The same was true of conferences in Detroit, San Diego, and so on. The remaining

10 percent from each conference is sent back to Promise Keepers' headquarters in Colorado to cover administrative costs. In 1996, Promise Keepers sponsored twenty-two such events in stadiums across the United States. When I pressed Chavis and his staff for a more specific breakdown of how PK disperses the huge amount of income from these conferences, my repeated requests received little response. But I had no real cause for suspicion. PK seems to have little to hide. In fact, Promise Keepers provides members of the media with a fact sheet showing its budget and offers an in-depth financial report to anyone who requests one.

The sheer numbers are impressive. PK's budget has been doubling almost every year. In 1994, according to its published figures, Promise Keepers' budget was $26 million, with a staff of 150 people; in 1995, PK had a budget of $65 million and employed 250 staff members; by 1996, the budget had grown to over $115 million with a paid staff of more than 400, not counting the thousands of volunteers who help make the organization run.

In 1995, according to PK's audited financial statement, Promise Keepers took in an additional $8.6 million in donations, over and above the cost of conference registrations, and a whopping $14 million from sales of Promise Keepers hats, mugs, shirts, and other resource materials. PK books, CDs and tapes, and the PK magazine, *New Man*, added $800,000 in royalties to Promise Keepers' coffers. To put those figures in perspective, retail stores peddling many of the same products as Promise Keepers take in annual sales averaging around $750,000. Clearly, the cogs in the PK machine are well-greased with greenbacks.

Once inside the Pittsburgh stadium, it was easy to understand why Promise Keepers charged so much to attend their conferences. The rental costs for the stadium, the sound system, and the staging set PK back a pretty penny, not to mention the money needed to pay speakers, musicians, staff members, and professional security personnel. On top of that was the cost of a New Testament Bible and a box lunch handed out to each participant.

For the Pittsburgh event, Promise Keepers rented Three Rivers Stadium from Thursday through Sunday. The Teamsters Union kept a close watch on all setup and tear-down work, making sure that its members were compensated for every minute they were on the scene. Promise Keepers themselves had more than sixty staff members on site.

The massive sound system used at Promise Keepers events rivals that of most major rock-and-roll shows, with twenty-four huge loudspeakers flying high above each side of the stage. Other clusters of speakers provided sound behind the stage to accommodate overflow seating, and still more were strategically aimed to keep reverberation to a minimum. The echo-chamber sound that plagues most stadium public address systems, causing announcers to be almost incoherent to the spectators and creating a nightmare for national anthem singers, would not be a problem for Promise Keepers. Promise Keepers is, after all, in the communications business.

Eleven tractor trailers haul the mammoth Promise Keepers rented sound system and staging from one site to another. Two thirty-five-man crews, one on each side of the Mississippi, are entrusted with the responsibility of assembling the 110-foot-high stage bedecked with the Promise Keepers' multicolored insignia featuring artistic renderings of three men—one black, one white, and one reddish brown. Even a casual glance at the stage reminds the crowd that PK is striving to embrace racial diversity.

Besides the Promise Keepers staff, each stadium conference requires the help of as many as 3,500 volunteers. The volunteers do everything from clerical work to interpreting for the deaf to helping to feed the thousands of hungry men in less than forty-five minutes during the Saturday afternoon lunch break. At the 1996 Detroit conference, volunteers distributed boxed lunches to 72,000 men in twenty-five minutes. Most of the volunteers have attended one or more previous PK conferences. About 30 percent of the volunteers at most Promise Keepers events are women. Many volunteers give up family vacation time to work for free at Promise Keepers events. One such person is Don Couls, from Shelby, Michigan.

Don and his wife, Terri, gave up two weeks of their 1996 summer vacation to serve as PK volunteers in charge of food services at the Detroit and Indianapolis conferences. An industrial sales manager, with no prior background in food service, Don oversaw the feeding of the staff, volunteers, and sound and light crew members, as well as the thousands of attendees at the conferences. "Sure it's stressful," said Don, "but I love it. I can't sing or speak the way some of the talented people do who are on the platform, but I can serve behind the scenes. I know that I am having a part in something that is helping a lot of families, including mine."

Staff members and strategic volunteers move around the stadium by means of a fleet of golf carts; staffers stay connected to each other by a state-of-the-art communications system. Problems are quickly identified and solved with the minimum of hassle and angst. Having seen firsthand the backstage mania of many music artists about to put on a major production, I was amazed at how calm most of the PK staff members were as they went about their jobs. Promise Keepers president Randy Phillips explained that they have now done enough conferences that the PK staff has the details down to a science. Maybe so, but it seemed to me that a much more profound sense of peace pervaded the atmosphere than that which could be explained by sheer professionalism. My thoughts drifted back to the parking attendant's comment, "This isn't your ordinary bunch."

As I made my way to the field level of the stadium, an all-male choir was warming up onstage. Most of the members were men of color and all wore black T-shirts imprinted with the slogan REAL MEN SING REAL LOUD. A soft-rock band was tuning up and doing a final sound check at the same time. In spite of the cacophony, the expectation and excitement onstage were almost palpable.

The mood of the men in Three Rivers Stadium was nothing short of festive, reminiscent of a rowdy crowd at a Steelers football game eagerly waiting for the opening kickoff. Spontaneous cheers arose from the crowd, one section of men vying in friendly competition to outdo the cheers from another section. Stadium "waves" moved across the Three Rivers crowd, as masses of men rose to their feet, raised their arms, bellowed, and sat back down. Despite the fact that some of the men had driven all day to get there and had waited in the stadium for the conference to start for nearly two hours, complainers were not to be seen or heard. Conspicuously absent from the stadium scene were the ballpark beer vendors, but the Coca-Cola stand was doing a brisk business.

The crowd was a mixture; from men dressed in shorts and T-shirts appropriate for the warm summer evening, to guys in business suits who apparently came to the stadium straight from work, to the golf shirt and perfectly pressed slacks set. Promise Keepers seems to appeal to younger men, but many in the stadium were baby boomers and older. The largest percentage of the men were white; approximately 10 percent of the Pittsburgh crowd were "men of color": African American, Asian American, or Hispanic, which was fairly reflective of the demographics in the greater Pittsburgh area.

The music cranked up at precisely 6:30 P.M., led by Joseph Garlington, an African American pastor of an inner-city church in the Pittsburgh suburb of Wilkinsburg. Garlington was backed by a top-notch ensemble of musicians and singers, known as the Maranatha Promise Band. Across the stage, opposite the Promise Band, the Real Men choir sang, clapped their hands, and swayed to the rhythm of the music. The musical styles of the eclectic group leaned toward pop and soft rock, though the lyrical content was decidedly traditional. Whatever the label, the music was catchy. The men in the crowd were soon belting out old hymns as well as new choruses, the words of which were all displayed prominently on huge "Jumbotron" scoreboard screens.

Following the music, Tony Evans, a black pastor from Dallas, spoke to the men. The theme of the weekend, and of all Promise Keeper events in 1996, was "Break Down the Walls," so Evans talked of how the walls could be broken down between men and God, men and women, and men and their children.

More music followed, and then the founder of Promise Keepers, Bill McCartney, a bespectacled white man in his mid-fifties, took the stage. Trim, tanned, and athletic-looking in his casual golf shirt embroidered with a Promise Keepers logo (the standard uniform for all PK speakers), McCartney's more-than-six-foot frame made for an imposing figure standing behind the podium. As he usually does, the former football coach began his talk with a story leading to a humorous punchline. Having captured the crowd's attention, McCartney bored in on his topic, supposedly brokenness; but as McCartney is prone to do, he soon strayed from his advertised topic and plunged headlong into the issue of tearing down walls between religious denominations and races. Speaking slowly and methodically at first, his voice gradually escalated in pitch, volume, and intensity as he went along, sounding more and more like a coach on the sidelines yelling instructions to his players on the field.

McCartney's talk was replete with football stories, including the poignant tale of a second-team linebacker at the University of Illinois who begged his coach to let him play in the biggest game of the year. The coach finally consented and allowed the young man to start the game, and the second-teamer performed like an All-Star, making spectacular plays throughout the game and leading the team to victory. After the game, the young man explained that his blind father had died a few days earlier and this game was the first time—looking down from heaven—that his dad could ever see him play.

As I listened to Bill McCartney conclude the story, and watched dads all over the stadium wipe tears from their eyes, it struck me that much of the Promise Keepers' message is steeped in sports imagery. PK speakers and leaders frequently relate being a better husband, father, and citizen to winning the big game or competing in the heat of battle. While some men—and women—may be alienated by all the sports talk, many more seem to feel that at last somebody is speaking about real-life issues in terms they understand. In Pittsburgh, for instance, McCartney encouraged the men to "put up high numbers" when it came to crossing racial and denominational barriers. The former coach's talk seemed to be well received by the majority of the men in the audience. He was interrupted several times by standing ovations.

The evening concluded at 10:00 P.M. sharp, just as the Promise Keepers program organizers had meticulously planned. Saturday would be a full day of more messages and music; no use wearing out the conferees on the first night.

Sure enough, by 6:30 A.M. the following morning, Three

Rivers Stadium once again began to fill with men, many of whom had spent the night sleeping on the floors of area churches after other Promise Keepers bought out every available hotel room in the city. Guys who ordinarily struggled to stay awake during their pastor's brief sermon back home listened enthusiastically to one speaker after another throughout the day. Few men left the stadium for long. When the afternoon sun heated the stadium tarp to a near-sizzle in the searing midsummer heat, many men removed their shirts, stretched out on the stadium floor, and caught some rays while they caught another inspiring message.

Into the afternoon the program went on. Despite the fact that no evening meal was served, the men stayed. Nobody wanted to miss what was sure to be a grand finale, an extravaganza of some sort.

But fireworks never happened. Instead, the weekend gathering drew to a close at six-thirty on Saturday evening with a low-key appeal for men who wanted God to change them—and make them into better husbands, fathers, and brothers—to come to the staging area to pray. The spontaneous outpouring of men flowing onto the tarp surprised even experienced Promise Keepers staff members. Watching from the press box area, Bill McCartney himself was in awe, as thousands of men poured onto the stadium floor. So many men responded that the chairs located on the field level were moved aside. Men began to kneel on the tarp, faces to the floor, weeping and calling out to God. By the time the flow of men from the stands to the stadium floor slowed, nearly the entire floor of Three Rivers Stadium was covered by men on their knees praying. Rather than ending in a round of "Let's go take on the world!" hype and hoopla, the Pittsburgh conference ended in a holy, reverent hush, sending the men back to their hometowns and families, ready to roll up their sleeves and make positive changes in their primary relationships and in the world.

One usually sardonic reporter in the press box turned to another writer who had been skeptical of Promise Keepers at the outset and said simply, "This is God."

The second man was me.

The following day, speaking at the World Links Conference in Pine Mountain, Georgia, McCartney said that what happened in Pittsburgh exceeded anything he had seen with Promise Keepers to date.[3]

More than forty-four thousand men had attended the event at Three Rivers. That's a crowd almost as large as the four-time Super Bowl champion Pittsburgh Steelers command for most games, and nearly twice as many people as the Pittsburgh Pirates pull even in the heat of a pennant race. And the Pittsburgh conference was one of the "smaller" crowds gathered in stadiums around the country in 1996 to hear the Promise Keepers' challenge to be better husbands, fathers, and citizens. Attendance at Promise Keepers events in 1996 averaged well above the fifty thousand mark.

Fifty thousand men standing and cheering in a packed-out stadium—what's so unusual about that? Nothing . . . until you recall that they are not cheering about some guy lugging an inflated hunk of pigskin across a bunch of white lines, or another guy trying to hit a cowhide-covered ball with a big stick. In fact, there's not even a ball in sight, unless you count the several oversized beachballs being bounced across the heads of unsuspecting onlookers during breaks in the action.

Whatever else you think, there is no escaping the enthusiasm. These guys cheer for God! They come from miles around—some as far as three states away—to learn how to better love God, their families, and their neighbors. And few can contest that the Promise Keepers movement has swept the United States like no spiritual renewal in the past one hundred years. Even the movement's most adamant critics must acknowledge that Promise Keepers is having a significant impact upon the men who attend.

But who are the Promise Keepers? Where and how was the organization birthed, and who is leading this grassroots return to time-honored concepts of manhood in a politically correct cultural climate? Is Promise Keepers a church? A political action group? A reactionary throwback to the male attitudes of the 1950s? Or is Promise Keepers a cutting-edge, spiritual power-saw, providing millions of men with the courage to rip against the grain of status quo concepts of what it means to be a man as we enter a new millennium?

Should contemporary males embrace Promise Keepers, or be embarrassed that such an organization exists? Are there any dangers about which men—and women—should be concerned, any pitfalls to be avoided? What happens to a man when he becomes a Promise Keeper? How do women respond to Promise Keepers? What difference does a Promise Keeper make in his family, and in the world at large? These are some of the questions that we will examine in this book. If you have wondered why anyone would get so excited about a bunch of men who simply want to keep their promises . . . keep reading. You might be surprised.

CHAPTER 2

A COACH'S DREAM

"Okay, guys; listen up. This is the big one. We've worked hard; we all know our jobs. We can do it. Never mind that the press is calling me a raving lunatic who has taken my wife for granted for three decades while I've chased my own dreams. Never mind that my own daughter has been impregnated twice by players on my own team. Never mind that I have not been the best example in some other areas of my life. The team I have trained is in excellent shape. We have a superlative playbook. We've hired some of the best assistant coaches and superstar players available, and I still know how to win. Now it's up to you. It's time to take charge of your family and society, and get out there and win this thing!"

An imaginary coach's pep talk? Of course. But not so far from reality as you might think. The above fictitious account could easily be attributed to the founder of Promise Keepers, Bill McCartney.

Like many controversial movements, Promise Keepers began simply, in relative obscurity. On March 20, 1990, Bill

McCartney, then head football coach at the University of Colorado, and his friend Dr. Dave Wardell, an assistant professor of physical education at the same school, were driving from Boulder to Pueblo, Colorado. The two were headed to a Fellowship of Christian Athletes banquet where McCartney was to speak. During the three-hour ride, McCartney and Wardell, both Christians, talked, sang, prayed, and listened to tapes of religious music and speakers. At one point in the trip McCartney asked Wardell, "If money were not an issue and you could do anything you wanted with your life, what would you do?"

Wardell did not have to think long before saying he would work with men on a one-to-one basis, helping them to develop a strong relationship with God. McCartney was intrigued. When Wardell asked the coach the same question, McCartney revealed a strikingly similar dream, one he had been entertaining for some time. "I envision men coming together in huge numbers . . . worshiping and celebrating their faith together. I long to see men openly proclaiming their love for Christ and their commitment to their families."[1]

The two men began to share their dreams quietly with close friends. As more and more friends caught the vision for a new men's movement, McCartney set to work networking. Soon he had gathered an eclectic cadre of seventy men who agreed to meet to pray about mobilizing men around a spiritual focus rather than politics, sports, or career interests. The "Seventy" not only received McCartney's idea with enthusiasm, they set out to recruit other men, as well. Each member of the group committed himself to pray for a spiritual stirring among men in America. Each linked their prayers with occasional fasting. Moreover, they began to plan for a conference—what was to become the first Promise Keepers conference—to be held in Colorado.

The name "Promise Keepers" was also chosen in a somewhat epiphanic fashion. "Coach Mac," as he is still often called, and his associates wanted their group to be known for their personal and corporate integrity. When they looked up the word *integrity* in the dictionary, they found that its meanings included "utter sincerity, moral soundness, honesty, and candor, with nothing artificial and no empty promises." They concluded that "a man of integrity is a man who keeps his promises."[2] The idea resonated with the men, and Promise Keepers they became.

In July 1991, the first Promise Keepers conference in Boulder, Colorado, drew more than 4,200 men. After that, McCartney and his men began to dream of filling Folsom Stadium, the University of Colorado's football facility. In July 1992, more than 22,500 men gathered at Folsom Stadium to hear speakers teach them how to be better husbands, fathers, and leaders. The following year, McCartney's dream came true: Promise Keepers assembled 50,000 men in Folsom Stadium, filling it to capacity. At the close of the 1993 conference, one thousand pastors from a wide variety of denominations converged at the front of the stadium to recommit themselves as spiritual leaders. Meanwhile the men in the stands affirmed their appreciation of the pastors by cheering wildly, giving the pastors a prolonged standing ovation, and shouting in unison, "We love you!"

In his closing comments that night, Bill McCartney hinted at his goals for the fledgling movement when he asked, "What would it be like if a stadium full of men in each state across the country began to take God at his word?" Although Promise Keepers did not come close to a conference in each state in the year that followed, the seven conferences they did sponsor in 1994 brought together more than 275,000 men. Since then, attendance at Promise Keepers conferences has skyrocketed; 724,342 men filled stadiums in thirteen cities in

1995, and more than a million men attended Promise Keepers conferences in twenty-two cities in 1996. In both Los Angeles and Detroit, Promise Keepers packed more than 70,000 men into football stadiums.

Why do the men come? At the Promise Keepers conference in Indianapolis, I stopped a guy wearing a fluorescent lime-green hat, just like twenty or thirty others bobbing through the crowd. I figured he'd have no trouble spotting the other members of his group if he got separated. "Why are you here?" I asked the man.

"I don't know," he answered. "The other guys from my church were coming, so I decided to come along." Then, rather sheepishly, he added, "Besides, my wife says this might be good for me." He hurried off to rejoin the other fluorescent-lime hats.

A former college football player simply wanted to hear Bill McCartney in person. "I've admired the coach for his success at the University of Colorado, and I've tried to follow him in the press since he first started Promise Keepers," he told me. "I've read a lot about him, but this will be my first chance to ever hear him give an entire speech. I've heard that Coach Mac doesn't mince words at these sessions. I like that."

When I asked a muscular black man why he had come, his reply was more mystical. "Brother," he said as he laid his hand on my shoulder, "you haven't lived until you've sung 'Amazing Grace' with a stadium full of men." A white man with a pronounced paunch was much more down-to-earth in his explanation of why he was attending the Promise Keepers conference. "My wife of eighteen years is ready to file for divorce, my teenage daughter wants to drop out of school and run off with her boyfriend, and I can't handle much more stress. I'm hoping I can pick up some pointers here that will help me save my family before it is too late."

Whatever the varied reasons for the attraction to Promise Keepers, unquestionably one of the main motivations given by attendees is the opportunity openly to discuss issues that trouble them, away from the knowing glances of their wives, mothers, sisters, or girlfriends. Many men, especially baby boomers and younger men, welcome the opportunity to talk about the confusion they are experiencing concerning their male identity, especially regarding what a modern man should look, sound, act, and feel like. Much of the frustration centers around men trying to sort out their role in the modern family. Today most men hold much different attitudes toward male and female roles than their parents or grandparents did. Many no longer believe that specific roles are valid at all, yet a suspicion that something is out of whack continues to gnaw at them. Many of these men show up at Promise Keepers, looking for answers.

"I was raised to believe that the man should be in charge of the family," said Paul, a winsome insurance agent from Virginia who attended the Washington, D.C., Promise Keepers conference. "My sisters and I gave my daddy respect simply because he was our father. He worked hard to put clothes on our backs and food on the table, so a lot of our decisions revolved around what made life easier for Daddy. Mama managed most of the housework and was the heart of our home, but Daddy was the head. He didn't have to serve us or earn our gratitude. We just knew he was the boss in our home.

"Today, my wife is a pilot with a major airline. She doesn't have dinner on the table when I get home from work. Matter of fact, she's usually not home when I get home. I drop our kids off at day care on the way to my job and I pick them up at night. In the back of my mind, I have an image of what it means to be the head of our home, but I have no illusions of ever being that sort of man. And I wonder, 'Am I a failure because I cannot be the same sort of leader my daddy was?'

"At Promise Keepers, I met a bunch of other guys who were once just as confused as I was, but who had now found some answers. We want to be sensitive, caring men, but we don't want to be emotionally emasculated to do it. Promise Keepers is showing us how to sort through those issues and address them in positive ways."

Promise Keepers emphasizes specific roles for a husband and father to play, roles that encourage the man to stand up and lead his family rather than sit back and be pushed or pulled around by society's politically correct images of what the family should be. Men by thousands are responding positively to PK's message. Many of them echo the sentiments of Gregg, a young business executive from St. Petersburg who said, "I've always felt that I should be assuming the leadership role in my family. But for a variety of reasons I have believed that I would be considered an egotistical dictator if I tried to operate in my family that way nowadays. Promise Keepers not only gives me permission to do what I have felt to be right, but encourages me and shows me practical ways to do it without offending my wife."

Besides validating men's latent desires for leadership roles, Promise Keepers fortifies the hope in men that they can stand against what many perceive as the sliding sludge caused by the erosion of values in society. Increasing violence, mounting racial tensions, weakening marriage vows, exasperating problems relating to drug addictions, premarital pregnancies, sexual immorality, and divorce are all flashing signs to many Promise Keepers, warning that society is on a headlong course toward destruction. Out of this moral quagmire in our culture, Promise Keepers has arisen to offer something to men who are seeking help in developing or maintaining strong ethical values. Many men in the stadiums look to Bill McCartney himself as a role model in these areas. They identify with the coach and seem to respond to his inspiring rhetoric. They say, "If Coach Mac can stand against the tide, I can, too."

While PK heavily emphasizes a man's taking responsibility and being a "real man," I was surprised to discover that one of the most underrated aspects of a Promise Keepers conference is the sheer fun the men have while they are together. Outside the stadium, guys are laughing, telling jokes, tossing Frisbees, and goofing off in ways many of them have not done since their school days. Inside, during a break, inevitably somebody launches a Styrofoam airplane from the upper decks, although Promise Keepers officially frowns upon this, and its emcees repeatedly discourage such actions (more for insurance reasons, no doubt, than any attempt to dampen the frivolity). The plane floats across the stadium even longer than thought possible, seemingly buoyed by the enthusiastic cheers of the men-turned-boys in the crowd. The plane is tossed around the stadium, from one section to the next, until it somehow or other makes its way back to the upper decks to await the countdown for its next launch.

And then there are the ubiquitous beach balls . . . The men stow the balls safely out of sight during most of the keynote addresses. The majority of the audience members at most Promise Keepers events are extremely attentive and respectful of the platform speakers while they are presenting their messages. But at the first sign of a break in the action, the stadium suddenly sprouts beach balls everywhere. The balls bounce freely across the heads and shoulders of guys. Most men simply swat them away good-naturedly. Others go after them with a vengeance, whacking a ball high into the air and laughing uproariously as it bounces off some unsuspecting fellow's nose. Clearly, Promise Keepers not only encourages men to be men, but the PK experience also allows men to be boys—expressing their playful sides.

Speakers at Promise Keepers sometimes lead in the antics, as when noted author and Dallas Theological Seminary president Charles Swindoll, dressed in a faded denim outfit, rode into Folsom Stadium on a Harley-Davidson motorcycle while the 1960s rock and roll hit "Born to Be Wild" blasted from the sound system. The men in the audience loved it, roaring their approval through their laughter. Later that evening, Gary Smalley, another well-known author and speaker, hilariously made his entrance on a kiddie-sized Big Wheel bike, again to the boisterous crowing of the crowd. Promise Keepers may have plenty of poignant, serious moments, but their conferences are definitely not stuffy. That factor itself may attract many men to PK events.

Beyond that, many men long for vulnerable, accountable relationships with other men; relationships in which a guy can spill his guts and admit his frustrations, insecurities, and failures without fear of condemnation or public exposure. The Promise Keepers movement offers hope of such an experience.

Most of all, Promise Keepers provides a man a communal, very public avenue in which to be vulnerable, while in a "safe" environment, with thousands of other guys who are willing to be equally open. Although it defies logic, for some reason these men feel it is safe to let down their guard in front of thousands of other men in a stadium, yet many of them have never done this with the women they love, or in a local church atmosphere. At Promise Keepers functions it is not unusual to see men hugging one another, praying with or for each other, crying together, and pouring out their hearts to one another. When was the last time something like that happened at work, at the club, or even in church? And what man would not welcome the support of some guys who will not make fun of him for his insecurities, fears, failures, and will encourage him to overcome the transient and unfulfilling temptations of power, money, and sex so highly touted by our modern society, and to invest his life in his family?

Stephen, a computer analyst from the Chicago area, summed up his attraction to Promise Keepers. "At Promise Keepers, during the huge stadium conferences, and also back home with a small group of guys at my church—not in my church at large, but with a few guys I can trust—I can be free to be weak. Why? Because I know the other guys will encourage me. I can admit my failures without fear of condemnation or reprisal. My Promise Keepers group is like an oasis in a desert."

Promise Keepers encourages a guy to develop his spiritual side; to make improving his relationship with his wife a priority; to maintain moral and sexual purity; to be a faithful and committed father to his children; to seek out and maintain close male friends; to actively support his local church; to break down racial and denominational barriers; and to encourage other guys to do the same. What could possibly be wrong with that?

Yet all is not milk and honey in the land of Promise Keepers. The movement has evoked the ire of plenty of detractors. It has been assailed by feminist groups, the American Civil Liberties Union, and liberal politicians. It has received both friendly fire and blistering blasts from fundamentalist Christian groups who claim that McCartney's brand of ecumenicalism goes against the teachings of the Bible.

Bill McCartney has been somewhat of a controversial figure in Colorado, largely because of his religious beliefs. He was revered by some and reviled by many in the University of Colorado community of Boulder. While McCartney led the

Colorado Buffaloes to a national collegiate football title in 1990, he received scathing rebukes for his outspoken style of mixing sports and Christianity. The Jewish watchdog group, the Anti-Defamation League, accused him of using his state-tax-funded coaching position as a pulpit for his personal beliefs. McCartney's strong encouragement of his players to attend chapel services and participate in pregame prayers prompted the American Civil Liberties Union to threaten the university with a lawsuit.

McCartney's personal beliefs most rankled his critics when, at a 1992 press conference, the coach called homosexuals "an abomination against Almighty God." McCartney's open support for "Amendment 2," a confusing 1992 Colorado state ballot question that refused to give gays special treatment under the law, had drawn salvos of criticism from gay-rights activists. When it had become known that Coach Mac had permitted Colorado for Family Values, one of the bill's key sponsors, to use his name in its fund-raising letters, the university received complaints about the conflict between McCartney's highly publicized personal views and his position as coach at a state university supported by taxpayers. Coach McCartney agreed to ask the sponsor of Amendment 2 to cease using his name, and called a press conference to make the announcement. It was there that he uttered his now-infamous remark about gays being an abomination against God.

Similarly, McCartney's pro-life, anti-abortion beliefs drew catcalls in Colorado as well, particularly when the coach showed up as guest speaker at Operation Rescue functions. Liberal Colorado Congresswoman Pat Schroeder publicly called McCartney a "self-appointed ayatollah."

In a largely derogatory article in *GQ* magazine, writer Scott Raab referred to Coach McCartney as a "raving lunatic," and likened his influence over the men who attend Promise Keepers conferences to that wielded by Adolph Hitler over the crowds in pre–World War II Germany. Raab concluded, "There's nothing new, much less revolutionary, in what Promise Keepers is pushing, which is not really about Jesus Christ at all, but about Satan. After listening to all the speeches and the prayers, after reading their books and magazines, it's abundantly clear that these guys see the Archenemy everywhere, but especially in the mirror. What PK offers men finally is protection—from themselves."[3]

McCartney himself has been castigated for being a dubious role model in an organization proclaiming family and moral values to be priorities. Besides admitting to past battles with alcohol and his temper, McCartney is quick to acknowledge his own failure to keep his family priorities straight, not only before the inception of Promise Keepers, but afterward as well. His relationship with his wife, Lyndi, was severely damaged in the process.

McCartney admits to neglecting Lyndi while building his own reputation as a premier college football coach. Coaching demanded much of McCartney's time and took him away from Lyndi regularly. If "Coach's" wife thought things would change after husband Bill became involved in Promise Keepers, she was sorely disappointed. Instead of bringing the couple together, they were apart more than ever. Lyndi confessed:

> I never enjoyed sharing my husband. I always felt cheated. So many times Christians would send me cards or flowers, writing lovely letters saying how much they appreciated me sharing my husband with them. Sometimes my unChristian spirit would take over and

I'd want to tell them to "quit borrowing my husband." I really did not like sharing him so much, and I began to resent it. People were always poking into our lives, stealing Bill's time, and I was so angry with him because he would let them do it . . .[4]

McCartney's wife eventually became exasperated to the point of nearly giving up on trying to win her husband back from his dual mistresses of pigskin and Promise Keepers. She was not opposed to the work Coach Mac was doing, but she wanted "Husband Mac" to give her some of the time and attention he so freely shared with so many other people. Finally, Lyndi closed the door and pulled down the shades in her life, sealing herself in and her husband Bill out. Lyndi recalls, "I spent about a year in isolation. The kids were out and on their own, and there were just the two of us in the house. I didn't answer the telephone, and I shut the door on all outsiders. I even shut out friends who loved me. I thought I needed time to myself, time with my husband, to see if we could salvage our lives."[5]

In recent years, Bill McCartney has been quick to assume full responsibility for the demise of his relationship with Lyndi. Lyndi, however, will not allow him to wallow alone in contrition and self-abnegation. She recognizes that although she has been hurt by her husband's inconsideration, her response to the pain he inflicted was destroying their marriage and her as a woman. She admitted:

I had to confront my own bitterness. I was hopelessly caught, eyebrow deep, in pain and blind to all the good; I was a wounded, ugly woman. I had made my husband my god and my Savior my sidekick. My life was bleeding profusely, and I was experiencing the consequences of worldly living, and failing my loving Savior.

I read more than a hundred books in 1993. I read book after book on recovery, on healing and on restoration. More importantly, I read the Bible constantly.[6]

Lyndi's emotional and spiritual depression took a physical toll on her body. She lost seventy pounds that year, thirty of them in January alone. But it wasn't Lyndi's weight loss that captured Coach McCartney's attention. It was the look in her face. One day the couple was listening to Jack Taylor, a guest speaker in their home church, when the preacher said, "Do you want to know about a man's character? All you need to do is look into his wife's face, and everything that he has invested or withheld will be in her countenance."

McCartney took the challenge and looked into Lyndi's face. What he saw shattered him. Despite being the leader of a movement that stated as one of its goals the primacy of marriage, McCartney suddenly realized that his own marriage was in dire need of attention. He later said, about looking in Lyndi's face, "After thirty-one years, all I saw was pain . . . I didn't see contentment, I saw torment." The vibrant glow that had once graced his wife's face was long gone.

Lyndi McCartney recalls:

I kept things inside for so long. I didn't let Bill see my pain. When it all came gushing out, I'm sure he was surprised—even shocked—at some of the things I had to say. I told him I needed to be on his calendar, so he began penciling me in. But then I got erased a couple of times. So I went back and told him I wanted to be written in ink—"It's ink or nothing," I said. I think he got the message.[7]

Loud and clear. Within two weeks after seeing the pain in Lyndi's face, and recognizing that it was largely his fault,

McCartney got down on his knees before her and asked her if she could forgive him. She did, but not immediately. Only as the McCartneys, and especially Coach Mac, concentrated on rebuilding their own marriage did the glow return to Lyndi's face. In the process, Bill McCartney was humbled, humbled before God and the woman he believed that God had given to him.

To many critics, more telling than the McCartneys' marriage problems was Coach's inability to pass on the moral values he espoused to his own daughter, Kristyn. During McCartney's tenure at the university, his daughter became pregnant twice outside of marriage. In both pregnancies, the fathers of Bill McCartney's grandchildren were players on his football team. In 1988, the father of Kristyn's first baby was Sal Aunese, McCartney's star quarterback of Samoan descent who died of cancer on September 23, five months after the birth of Timothy Chase. Although Aunese at first had contested his paternity of Kristyn's child, and only acknowledged his responsibility after a blood test, Coach McCartney spoke at Sal's funeral and honored both Aunese and Kristyn for not having an abortion, but choosing to allow T.C. to be born.

Then in 1993, just prior to the crisis in Bill and Lyndi McCartney's marriage, their daughter Kristyn became pregnant again, at age twenty-four, this time by McCartney's defensive tackle Shannon Clavelle, also a man of color. Whether Kristyn's second pregnancy by one of McCartney's team members influenced what happened next, or merely exacerbated an already crumbling homelife, is sheer conjecture, perhaps even for the coach. McCartney rarely discusses in public his daughter's second pregnancy, though in an interview with *Sports Illustrated* he "freely admitted that he neglected his children—he and Lyndi also have three sons—as they were growing up, instead spending all his time 'with someone else's kids.' " McCartney implied in the interview that if he had been around more, maybe things would have turned out differently for Kristyn. "Later, when told what her father had said, Kristy sighed and said, 'I would say that's right. We missed out on a lot.' "[8]

Regardless, on November 19, 1994, Bill McCartney gave up his $350,000-per-year contract—a deal in which he still had ten years remaining—and resigned as head coach of the Colorado Buffaloes. Many of McCartney's longtime critics had lobbied for him to be fired; few ever thought the coach would quit.

Bill McCartney renewed his promises to his family and decided to devote his life to helping develop other Promise Keepers. On July 1, 1995, he began working full-time with the organization he had helped birth, but from which he had previously taken no salary. McCartney's official PK title became that of "founder"; then, in 1996, McCartney became Promise Keepers' chief executive officer. Randy Phillips, Promise Keepers' first and only president to date, and the other top-level leaders of PK have remained in their positions, while McCartney functions as the organization's most familiar and visible public figurehead. Although he receives an honorarium when he speaks at a PK conference, McCartney still accepts no salary.

According to Bill McCartney, before one of the final Promise Keepers events in 1995, Lyndi told him, "Bill, when you talk to the men at the rallies, be sure to tell them the glow is back."

He does. And the guys hear him. The coach is, after all, someone they can identify with—both a tough guy who had led his football team to a national championship and a man who had failed bitterly in the arena of his family relationships. The men in the stadiums understand; many of them have sacrificed their families on altars of ambition, and similar to Bill McCartney, they are now ready to learn how to be better husbands and fathers.

Despite the naysayers and the McCartney bashers, the Promise Keepers movement is far too significant to be discounted as simply another religious flash in the pan, or the pet cause of an inspiring founder and leader. The movement is complex, and may hold the potential to transform the fabric of contemporary society. On a personal level, it might change you.

That's why it is important for you to know what the Promise Keepers really believe.

CHAPTER 3

PROMISES, PROMISES

For many of us, the concept of promise keeping sounds unrealistic. We are much more accustomed to the idea of promise *breaking*. From the ephemeral promises of politicians, to contracts that are broken and renegotiated regularly in business, to the sports team that wants to move its franchise to another city after the taxpayers have shouldered enormous burdens to support it, we are no longer surprised when somebody does not keep his or her word. Promise breaking has become almost expected. Let someone express a sincere desire to keep a promise and eyebrows raise immediately in surprise, skepticism, or disbelief.

In such an environment, Promise Keepers challenges modern-day men to commit themselves to keeping not merely one difficult promise, but seven. No wonder eyes are rolling!

Yet these guys are serious. As renowned radio preacher and president of Dallas Theological Seminary Charles R. Swindoll reminded tens of thousands of men at a 1994 conference in Anaheim, "This is called Promise Keepers, not just promise makers."[1]

From the earliest days of its organization, the leaders of Promise Keepers were convinced that many of society's ills could be linked to broken promises. Broken treaties, broken marriage vows, and broken commitments in business and the community all yield the same results: a lack of confidence and security that leads to anger, resentment, and even violence.

They realized that they must begin by admitting their own failures. They acknowledged that it is not just "those guys" who have broken promises. It is "us guys, too"—men, claiming to be Christians, who have reneged on their promises and damaged relationships between husbands and wives, parents and children, and within society at large.

The leaders of Promise Keepers began to assemble some statements to summarize just what it means to be a Promise Keeper. Their basic premise rested on a solid Old Testament foundation in which God is described as a promise keeper: "God is not a man, that he should lie, nor a son of man, that he should change his mind. Does he speak and then not act? Does he promise and not fulfill?" (Numbers 23:19 NIV). Simply put, God keeps his word.

Mortal men don't do nearly so well in that department, but the leaders of Promise Keepers decided that the passage suggests a laudable goal. They discussed how being a Promise Keeper might transform a man's relationship to God, to his spouse and family members, to his friends and coworkers, to his community, and to his world. Eventually they distilled their findings into seven basic statements that describe the essence of what it is to be a Promise Keeper.

That there are seven promises is no accident. Many students of biblical numerology regard seven as a symbol of perfection, the number of wholeness and completion. Promise Keepers claims no such perfection or completeness for its seven promises. Many areas of life are not directly addressed at all; others are given only passing notice. For instance, none of the promises deal with work issues, including how a man obtains and uses his money; no promise speaks specifically to the redefining of the family unit, despite an increasing number of single parents in society. Nor are controversial matters such as gay marriage, euthanasia, conception questions, or "quality of life" issues mentioned.

These promises, however, were never intended to hold the same weight as Scripture or compete with the church creeds. Indeed, the seven promises of a Promise Keeper are not so much a new creed as they are a list of goals men can pursue throughout their lives. Promise Keepers president, Randy Phillips, says, "These promises are not designed as a new list of commandments to remind us of how badly we're doing with respect to the often-competing demands of the marketplace, the home, and the [international] mission field. Rather, they are meant to guide us . . . to transform us within so that we might see transformation in our homes, among our friends, in our churches, and ultimately, in our nation."[2]

Nevertheless, the seven promises do encompass several major areas with which modern men are dealing. The first three promises have to do with an individual's ethics and conduct. The last four promises focus on a man's relationship to a group and to society at large. These promises are not merely passive philosophical precepts. They demand action.

SEVEN PROMISES
IN A SOUND BITE

In their simplest form, the seven promises PK encourages men to keep are:

INDIVIDUAL ETHICS

1.
Trust in Christ.

2.
Form a few close male friendships.

3.
Practice moral and sexual purity.

SOCIETAL ETHICS

4.
Love your wife and children.

5.
Support your local church.

6.
Overcome racial and denominational prejudice.

7.
Encourage other men to do likewise.

PROMISE ONE

> ***A Promise Keeper is committed to honoring Jesus Christ through worship, prayer, and obedience to God's Word in the power of the Holy Spirit.***

It is impossible to truly understand the Promise Keepers phenomenon without recognizing that it is unabashedly Christian at its core. Promise Keepers regard Jesus as the "Ultimate Promise Keeper." Although Jesus never married, parented children, or ran for public office, his example of self-effacing love, uncompromising integrity, and willingness to sacrifice himself for the good of others are qualities extolled by Promise Keepers.

"**W**e're not trying to hide anything from these guys," one Promise Keepers mid-level official told me as he waved toward the men in the stadium with a sweeping motion of his arm. "We're right up front with them; we want them to know that we are talking about Jesus here. Like most Christians, we believe that if we all followed Jesus' example and lived by his instructions, the world would be better for it."

For example, Christians believe that Jesus was always true to his word. There is no record of him telling a lie; he never cheated anyone, nor did he ever make a promise he did not keep. His best friends, the twelve disciples, lived with him for nearly three years. They were with him during times of tremendous public acceptance, as well as times of extreme personal danger and stress. At the end of three years, the disciples—to a man—expressed the opinion that Jesus the pri-

vate person was identical to the persona he presented in public. Even Judas, the man who betrayed Jesus for thirty pieces
of silver, had to admit that Jesus' personal integrity was unas-
sailable.

Nor could Jesus' enemies sully his character. When a
group of religious leaders sought to get rid of Jesus, they could
find no credible witnesses to bring a charge against him. According to the New Testament, they bribed a few less-than-
respectable characters to distort Jesus' teachings so he could
be convicted and put to death on charges of trying to over-
throw the Roman government.

During his ministry years, Jesus had repeatedly predicted
the events surrounding his death, burial, and resurrection.
His disciples, however, did not catch on to what he was telling
them. When Jesus rose from the dead, on what we now call
Easter Sunday, his followers were as surprised as anyone.
Only then did his family, friends, and followers realize that
Jesus had kept his promises to them. And the confidence they
received from seeing Jesus back from the dead eventually
forged their faith, enabling them to believe everything else he
had taught them, including his promise that upon his depar-
ture, he would send the "Comforter," the Holy Spirit, to help
them.

A few days later, Jesus ascended into heaven and the Holy
Spirit came upon one hundred and twenty of Jesus' followers—just as he had promised—energizing them with a spiritual power such as the world had never seen. They were now
ready to take Jesus' message that although men and women
everywhere have failed to live up to God's standards, he loves
them, and wants them to be reconciled to him.

Thus, today's Promise Keepers believe that their primary
purpose is to honor Jesus. By honoring him, Promise Keepers
do not mean simply to acknowledge him as a great moral

teacher, or as a prophet. They mean to accept him as God, to trust him with their lives, and to accept his teachings as authoritative for daily living. In the PK book *The Awesome Power of Shared Beliefs*, Jeff Van Vonderen succinctly states Promise Keepers' position regarding Jesus: "Jesus Christ is the personal self-revelation of God . . . God is a personal being; if you want to see what that Person 'looks' like, acts like, and cares about, look at Jesus."[3]

That is why every Promise Keepers stadium conference opens with an old hymn, such as "All Hail the Power of Jesus' Name" or "Crown Him with Many Crowns," or another song that highly exalts Jesus Christ. That also explains why the opening speaker at each open-to-the-public conference always presents an evangelistic message, followed by a traditional "altar call," in which men are invited to respond to what they have heard, and take the first step toward becoming a Christian or renewing their Christian commitment. Though the language of the altar call may differ—black pastor Tony Evans invited the men in Pittsburgh to "come home" to their heavenly father; Illinois-based evangelist Michael Silva urged the men of Indianapolis to discover their "connectedness with God"; other speakers encourage the men to seek forgiveness for past sins and start over with God at the center of their lives—the message remains largely the same.

The attendees are encouraged to grapple with such issues as "What does it really mean to be a Christian? How can you know for sure that when you die, you will go to heaven?" If the men are not certain of their status with God, they are encouraged to admit their spiritual need—to admit, "I am a sinner. I have broken my promises to God, to my family, and to my world." They are instructed to repent—to turn away from their sins and turn toward God, seeking his help to live according to biblical principles. All of this is predicated upon the belief that Jesus died on the cross to pay the penalty for humankind's sins, and that by accepting what God has done for us, we can be forgiven. A person can "receive Christ into my life" by trusting him "by faith," regardless of the presence—or lack of—emotional or physical indicators. When I asked one man who had ostensibly found Jesus at a PK conference how he knew that he was "saved," he replied emphatically, "God made me an offer I couldn't refuse and I accepted it."

Inevitably, when this sort of invitation is given at a Promise Keepers event, men respond in huge numbers. In 1995 at the Silverdome in Pontiac, Michigan, following a message by internationally known evangelist Luis Palau, more than seven thousand men converged on the stadium's artificial flooring to ask Jesus Christ to direct their lives. At the Minneapolis Metrodome in July of that same year, following a message by John Wesley White, so many men responded to the opening invitation that the stadium aisles and tunnels were clogged. In the midst of the massive movement toward the front staging area, many men never reached the stadium floor before the program resumed, so they simply stopped in their tracks on the concession concourses, prayed, and committed themselves to being followers of Jesus Christ.

"You have to start with Jesus," a Promise Keepers "Evangelism Volunteer" told me as he and I watched nearly two thousand men stream to the front of the RCA Dome in Indianapolis in response to an appeal by Michael Silva, the first speaker at the 1996 Indy conference. "If you don't understand that this movement is about Jesus, all the rest of this talk about keeping our promises is mere gibberish."

Many of the men who respond to these public invitations

are doing so for the first time in their lives. Something about being in a stadium filled with men makes many participants more willing to walk the aisles than they traditionally have been at church or at other types of evangelistic crusade events.

Other men are seeking to clarify their relationship to God. "I just wanted to make sure everything was okay between God and me," said Manuel, a Hispanic attendee who responded to the altar call at the Washington, D.C., Promise Keepers conference. "I went to church all my life, but I never truly felt that I experienced God, until now. My relationship with God was based on fear and intimidation. I thought God was out to get me for all the bad things I had done. Now, I know he loves me; he has forgiven me, and he wants to help me to be the man he created me to be."

Experiencing this sort of crisis conversion at a Promise Keepers stadium conference can be heady stuff. Steve, a computer salesman in his mid-twenties, responded to Tony Evans's invitation to meet Jesus in Pittsburgh's Three Rivers Stadium. Steve trekked from the upper tier of the stadium, down several flights of stairs, and across the artificial turf of the stadium floor to the front of the staging area. By the time he got to the front, nearly a thousand other men had also gathered. Meanwhile the men in the stands were standing and applauding, giving the spiritual seekers a prolonged, thunderous ovation.

Steve later gushed, "What a rush! To think I invited Jesus to take control of my life while thousands of guys were giving me a standing ovation for doing it. Talk about positive peer pressure!"

Once the issue of spiritual allegiance is settled, Promise Keepers are encouraged to honor Jesus through worship.

Promise Keepers does not necessarily tell men how, when, or where to worship, but does encourage men to express their praise and adoration of God verbally. While at times worship may take the form of solitude and quiet contemplation, enthusiastic corporate worship (with the same exuberance once reserved for football games) is a major part of any Promise Keepers conference, and is one of the movement's main attractions to men who are accustomed to a more staid or stuffy form of worship, or none at all. It also produces some of the most lasting results in many men's lives, for when they leave Promise Keepers functions, they often incorporate a more visible and vocal form of worship in their homes and especially in their churches. After attending a Promise Keepers conference, many men are no longer content to sing songs *about* God; they want to sing *to* God in praise and worship.

Worship at a Promise Keepers event is most frequently loud, raucous singing of songs that praise Jesus directly, although the softer, quieter, more introspective forms of worship are not totally ignored. Amazingly, at Promise Keepers events, most guys do sing, and they sing loudly, even those who rarely vibrate their vocal chords in their home churches. Something mystical seems to happen as men dare to break through the sound barriers at Promise Keepers conferences. Even a skeptic might be moved by the awesome sound of seventy thousand male voices filling a stadium with the sounds of "Amazing Grace" or the gospel classic "How Great Thou Art." It is equally impressive to hear the men audibly praying. One is likely to feel a distinct impression that God is making himself known in the stadium as the men worship him. As one man said to me while we listened to the Promise Keepers worship, "I think God likes this a lot."

Leading newspapers and major magazines have published photographs depicting Promise Keepers with their hands raised, eyes closed, and faces radiantly lifted upward. Often the articles and captions accompanying such photos are mildly sarcastic and, at times, downright derogatory, giving the impression that these Promise Keeper types are other-worldly wackos. What the reporters and photographers some-times fail to understand is that the men are reverently lost in adoration of God. In a sense, the men have entered a spiritual oasis where, temporarily at least, they truly are "not of this world."

Prayer, too, plays a major role in the life of a Promise Keeper, not only at public conferences, but also in a man's personal and private life. At stadium conferences, the pro-gram often includes time for the men to pause and pray for each other. All over the stadium, groups of three and four men, some of whom may have just met, huddle together to pray for each man's needs. Moreover, one of the ongoing re-sults of Promise Keepers is the large number of men's prayer groups that have been formed on the local level. These groups continue long after the euphoria of a stadium event has dissi-pated. Promise Keepers are encouraged to return to their homes and continue to seek God in prayer for themselves, and to seek him with a group of men they can pray with on a regular basis.

"The best thing that happened to me as a result of going to a Promise Keepers event," said Jeff, a white-collar business executive, "is that I got invited to an early morning men's prayer group the following week. The group met at 6:00 A.M., so I wasn't too sure I wanted to be a part of it, but once I went, I was hooked. The guys get together with no other agenda but to pray for each other. We pray for our wives, our family needs, personal problems and opportunities, and a strengthening of our faith. I have never before known such care and concern from a group of guys."

Finally, Promise Keepers are committed to studying the Bible and applying its principles in their lives. Promise Keepers do not primarily read the Bible for historical or even inspirational information. They regard it as the road map for life, with truths that are nonnegotiable and meant to be obeyed. Promise Keepers are not hesitant to declare some things absolutely right or absolutely wrong, regardless of the circumstances, basing such decisions upon biblical principles.

While many men who become Promise Keepers have studied the Bible for years, others are discovering the Scriptures for the first time. Often they are astounded at how specific the biblical principles are. Jamie, a twenty-two-year-old unmarried college student who recently converted to Christianity at a Promise Keepers conference, expressed his surprise that the Bible forbids sexual intercourse before marriage and all sex outside the marriage relationship. He explained, "I have grown up with television and the movies, where if a guy and a woman care for each other, sex is a natural part of their relationship. Of course, I have always practiced discretion and safe sex because of the danger of AIDS, but I never dreamed in my wildest imagination that God had anything to say about sex. When I started studying the Bible with some of my Promise Keeper buddies, I was floored. I realized that I have been living contrary to God's plan for my life. I really want to do what is right, but it hasn't been easy. I've failed a few times and have given in to temptation, but the more I study the Bible, and the guys pray for me and with me, I know that with God's help, I can make it. The inner strength I need will come from God's Holy Spirit."

Clearly, Promise Keepers is much more than a "turn or burn" group of Bible thumpers. If all Promise Keepers provided was a male-oriented evangelistic thrust, it might have slipped into obscurity already. But what makes Promise Keepers so radically different from other previous efforts to mobilize men is its emphasis upon more than spiritual conversion. To Promise Keepers, spiritual conversion or renewal is the starting point, rather than the destination. Promise Keepers hope to transform society, and the plan by which they intend to do so is laid out in the remaining six promises.

CHAPTER 4

PROMISES TO EACH OTHER

Tony is a successful sales and marketing director for a nationally known company. He has a six-figure annual income, a gracious two-story colonial home in the suburbs, two expensive Mercedes-Benz automobiles, a gorgeous wife, and three wonderful children. Tony is highly respected in his church and in his community. By all appearances, Tony has it all. What Tony does not have is a friend.

"I just wish that I had one friend I could talk to without worrying that he was going to stab me in the back. I have areas of weakness in my life, areas where I am tempted and confused, and things that I just don't understand. Some days, I sit in my office fantasizing about having an affair with one of the attractive women with whom I work. Other days, I daydream about walking out of the office, getting in the car, pointing it toward someplace green and warm, and never coming back. I am weary of the pressure that comes with my work responsibilities and lifestyle. But I really don't dare talk with any of my colleagues about those things. Nor would I be willing to open up to most of the guys in my church. They all look to me for answers. They think I have it all together. They'd be shocked to discover just how lonely I really am."

Tony is not unique in his isolation. Although the reasons vary greatly, most modern men feel that they are cut off from meaningful interaction with other men. Not surprisingly, Promise Keepers strikes some nerves with its emphasis on men developing lasting friendships, strong personal convictions, a passion for personal integrity, and a willingness to make positive changes in their lives, all in the context of a small group of men in a local setting. Promise Two relates especially to the need of Promise Keepers like Tony.

PROMISE TWO

> *A Promise Keeper is committed to pursuing vital relationships with a few other men, understanding that he needs brothers to help him keep his promises.*

Looking at the nattily dressed men at a dinner party, or on an afternoon business flight where most of the seats are filled by travelers in dark suits and red ties, or seeing a group of guys at a football game, one might assume that the fellows are inseparably bonded together by their common maleness. But many adult men these days do not have close friendships with other men. Some guys do not have even one friend with whom they can be honest about what they feel deeply inside regarding their marriage, their job, or their future. Most men have a plethora of *acquaintances*, guys with whom they work or play golf, or with whom they may attend sporting events. But most men do not have another man with whom they feel comfortable looking in the eyes and saying, "Hey, I'm really hurting. Can I talk to you about it?" Instead, most men carry their inner pain alone.

Women, on the other hand, seem more able to be vulnerable with each other. They freely discuss with friends the intimate details of their lives, from their level of sexual satisfaction to their financial problems to their concern over serious social and spiritual issues. Men rarely open up to other men that way.

But Promise Keepers believe that they need to do so—desperately.

Promise Keepers tries to create an environment in which men can be open with one another without the fear that their confessions of need will come back to haunt them. Certainly this works best at the local levels, but it also takes place at the stadium conferences to some degree. Blaine, a rugged-looking man in his late forties, sat on a curb outside the Los Angeles Coliseum during the Saturday afternoon lunch break at the 1995 Promise Keepers conference. As he ate his boxed lunch along with two other men, Blaine began to open up on his concerns about his company's downsizing. "I've worked at this company for twenty years, and now without even as much as a thank you, they are going to lay me off. I don't know what to do. I don't have much of an education, and I'm too old to get a lot of the jobs the younger guys are doing. Frankly, I'm scared. I don't know how I am going to provide for my family. My wife is working odd jobs and trying to help out, but I can already see the stress taking a toll on her. She is exhausted all the time, impatient with our two teenagers, and short with me. And I feel like it is all my fault."

The men eating lunch with Blaine did not know how to solve his problem, but they provided something much more important—listening ears and hearing hearts. Blaine later revealed, "I have never admitted to anybody, ever, that I was afraid of anything. But just knowing that those guys cared about me and would pray with me gave me the confidence to open up and talk about some things I would not ordinarily express to anyone else, not even my wife."

As part of pursuing vital interaction with a few other men, Promise Keepers are encouraged to seek out mentoring relationships in their lives. Such relationships can impact a man long after he leaves the stadium conferences. Howard Hendricks is one of Promise Keepers' strongest advocates of mentoring. His definition of mentoring is similar to the ideal encouraged frequently in corporate America, as well as in many trades, the arts, and among skilled craftsmen. Hendricks believes that a mentor is a person who is willing to help others learn what he knows; how to do it and why it should be done.

Hendricks recommends that every man should have three significant mentoring relationships in his life. First, every Promise Keeper should have an older man to whom he can look for guidance, direction, and correction. Hendricks writes, "You need an older man who is willing to build into your life. Please note: not someone who's smarter than you are, not necessarily someone who's more gifted than you are, and certainly not someone who has life all together. That person does not exist. You need somebody who's been down the road. Somebody who's willing to share with you not only his strengths, but also his weaknesses. Somebody who's willing to share his successes and his failures—in other words, what he's learning in the laboratory of life."[1]

Second, Hendricks suggests that every man should have a man who is his peer, "a soul brother, somebody who loves you but is not impressed by you. Somebody who is not taken in by your charm and popularity and to whom you can be accountable."[2]

Third, Hendricks encourages men to seek out a younger man, somebody "into whose life you are building," someone who looks to you as the kind of person he wants to be. Hendricks implies that a man should have these three relationships happening simultaneously, rather than progressively.

How do Promise Keepers find these guys? They pray and look for them, as Hendricks urges. They ask God to bring men into their life with whom they can develop each of these relationships. Hendricks warns that a man should not be surprised if he does not hit it off with every other male in a mentoring relationship. Just as in marriage, harmonious relationships are not possible with any random pairing; not just any man will do when it comes to mentoring.

The second aspect of the Promise Keepers emphasis on developing strong relationships with a few men involves *accountability*. This concept is key to the long-term success of Promise Keepers. The idea is that a Promise Keeper should not even attempt to keep the seven promises alone; he needs other men to help him stick to his commitments. Two or three men are stronger together than as individuals, and despite men's tendency toward self-sufficiency—which results in most men being loners—men really do need other men to help them stay on track.

Specifically, what does Promise Keepers mean by "accountability"? On a personal level, Promise Keepers suggests that accountability means the willingness of a man to submit his life to a group, or to at least one other individual, to whom he grants the right to inspect key personal and professional matters. Certainly the group or person to whom he grants such a privilege should be competent and worthy of confidence and respect. These persons should demonstrate compassion and concern. They should help a man become answerable to them on some mutually determined, regular, and ongoing basis—in other words, a personal weekly checkup (or monthly, or at whatever frequency the Promise Keepers decide to meet). At this exam, the man grants accountability partners the right not only to inspect his life, but to expect him to explain his actions and attitudes; he grants them the right to offer advice, correction, encouragement, or rebuke, as often as necessary.

Promise Keepers as an organization recognizes the potential for abuse here by cautioning that accountability in moral, ethical, and spiritual matters should never be coercive. An accountability partner is not about *making* another do something. Questions such as should a man marry, what car he should buy, where he should go to church, or when he should have children are not given over to an authority figure. A Promise Keeper may seek advice in these matters, as most people do, but accountability does not confer on a group a "divine right" to speak authoritatively about intimate details of life.

PK would also caution that accountability to a group or individual should not replace accountability to a wife, boss, pastor, children, or the government. But Promise Keepers believe the optimum means of maintaining accountability is for men to be totally honest and uninhibited in expressing their hopes, dreams, fears, triumphs, or failures with a few men who will keep such sensitive matters confidential. The plurality of wisdom provided by a group of men may be of great benefit, since one man may be better qualified to keep another accountable in the realm of finances, for example, while someone else may have great wisdom in areas of marriage and family relationships. Many accountability groups have been spawned as a result of men returning from Promise Keepers conferences determined to develop accountable relationships.

Lacking an accountability group, a Promise Keeper can hope to find an accountability partner—one man with whom he will share his secrets, and who will have open access to his life, including freedom to ask the tough questions, such as:

Are you treating your wife the way you know you should?

Are you being totally faithful to your wife in your thoughts, as well as in more overt actions?

How much time have you been spending with your children?

Are you maintaining a positive mental attitude or are you dwelling upon negativism?

Are you watching or reading pornography?

Are you maintaining your integrity in the workplace?

Have you cut corners or compromised your honor in any way?

Are you misusing your influence in any way?

Are you eating a healthy, nutritious diet or are you surviving on sugar bursts?

How much time did you spend exercising this past week?

Are you having any problems with drugs, alcohol, or tobacco?

How is your relationship with God? How many chapters of the Bible have you read this week?

Are you spending time alone with God?

How much time this week did you dedicate to talking to God in private, specific prayer?

What is something you are really struggling with right now?

*   *   *

Some men have trouble understanding the need for an accountability group or partner. "Why would I want to have
somebody snooping around in my life, asking me such personal and private questions?" asked Peter, a man who had
started his own company and built it to a $6-million-per-year
business. "What I do on my own time is my business, and
nobody else's. Besides, I spent a good portion of my life working hard so I could become my own boss. Part of the reason I
started my own company was so I wouldn't have to answer to
anyone else. Why would I want to turn around and invite people to tell me what they think I am doing wrong?"

Granted, a man's building accountability into his life may
seem to go against his basic nature. Many men have never
seen a same-sex accountability partnership truly function. In
the past, relatively few men sought out such relationships.
Think about your own father, says Promise Keepers. To whom
was he accountable? Think about many of the highly publicized moral and financial failures that have been in the news
in recent years. To whom were these leaders accountable? PK
believes that one of the main reasons men get into trouble
financially, morally, or spiritually is because they have nobody
to whom they must give an account for what is going on in
their personal lives. The Internal Revenue Service may audit
their tax forms, quality-control personnel may oversee their
work, but who is examining the way they handle the most
important relationships of all—the way they deal with their
wives and children, and their personal relationships with
God?

Furthermore, accountability groups and partners need not
concentrate on what a man is doing wrong. Often the focus
can be on what is going right in one's life. The accountability
factor may provide the encouragement a man needs to take
the next step, to help him set realistic goals, to challenge him

to expand his horizons, or simply to help keep him on the right track. Ideally, an accountability relationship should be somewhat mutual, where both partners can help each other.

Promise Keepers founder Bill McCartney regards his promise to meet regularly with four other men as one of the most important commitments he has made as part of his renewed dedication to Lyndi and his children. Coach Mac says that he and his accountability partners study the Bible and pray during their time together. In this regard, McCartney is fond of quoting the Scripture: "As iron sharpens iron, so one man sharpens another" (Proverbs 27:17 NIV). In other words, just as one piece of strong metal can be used to sharpen another, one man can help sharpen the spiritual understanding and effectiveness of another when both are willing to hold each other to the fire in an accountable relationship.

PROMISE THREE

A Promise Keeper is committed to practicing spiritual, moral, ethical, and sexual purity.

More than any other of the seven promises, this one is the easiest to understand and perhaps the toughest to keep. Why? Because Promise Keepers are supposed to be men of integrity, men who do not set aside their faith as they leave the stadium conference or church property. Moreover, Promise Keepers are to live the way the Bible teaches, which includes adhering to such moral and ethical standards as those established in the Ten Commandments and Jesus' Sermon on the Mount.

Promise Keepers are to apply biblical principles in their work and business dealings as well as in their personal morality. In other words, a Promise Keeper should not cheat on his taxes, not simply because it is illegal, but because it violates God's commands that we should not steal and we should not tell a lie. A Promise Keeper will not fudge on his report to the stockholders because that, too, would be a compromise of the truth. A Promise Keeper will do what is right even when it affects the bottom line and is not "good for business." An employee who is a Promise Keeper will not use company copy machines, fax machines, or telephones for noncompany purposes. Nor will he pad the expense account or call in "sick" on days he spends hunting or out on the golf course. An employer who is a Promise Keeper will treat his employees with dignity, creating the best work environment possible and paying a fair wage. Regardless of whether it is popular or profitable, a Promise Keeper should do what is right.

Not only does becoming a Promise Keeper raise a man's standards of behavior, it raises other people's expectations of the man, as well. Sometimes that can be daunting. It was for Trent, a successful young graphic artist, who explains, "When I went to my first Promise Keepers conference, my buddy bought me one of the golf shirts with the Promise Keepers logo on the breast pocket, including the slogan, 'Men of Integrity.' I immediately put on the shirt while I was there. Back home, though, I was reluctant to wear the PK shirt, because guys in our slow-pitch softball league who knew about my temper outbursts and people who heard my language at work would be surprised to see me wearing a shirt with that statement. Besides, I felt that if I wore the shirt, people would be watching me, and I didn't want to let the Lord down or tarnish the image of Promise Keepers."

With or without the shirt announcing it, Promise Keepers are expected to be men whose outward actions reflect the faith they have within. What a Promise Keeper believes and how he acts should be synonymous.

* * *

Promise Keepers acknowledge that the aspect of Promise Three that is most susceptible to the influence of society's values is a man's commitment to sexual abstinence before marriage and sexual fidelity to his wife within marriage. Modern men (and women) find little cultural encouragement to maintain anything that could be classified as sexual purity.

Promise Keepers, however, have dared to buck the tide of popular sexual mores. Simply stated: Promise Keepers are not to have sex outside of marriage. Period. Basing their standards on the Bible, Promise Keepers are encouraged to have an active, healthy, happy sex life—but with one woman only, and that woman being the wife. At the 1994 Boulder Promise Keepers conference, John Maxwell, pastor of Skyline Wesleyan Church in San Diego, set the tone for sexual purity when he said, "God invented sex; it was his idea. Yeah, God! There is not a problem with sex as long as it is within its right bounds."[3]

To Promise Keepers, sexual purity implies more than merely avoiding sex with someone to whom one is not married. It also excludes the mental fantasies men might have through pornography. All vicarious sex outside of marriage, whether encouraged by books, magazines, videos, or the Internet, is discouraged by Promise Keepers. Indeed, helping men overcome sexual temptations, including those of pornography, is a major emphasis of the Promise Keepers' follow-up material known as "The Next Step," designed to help men move from the spiritual smorgasbord of the stadium conferences to a more steady spiritual diet provided through belonging to a small men's group back home.

Promise Keepers readily admit that living a life of sexual purity is not easy; but, they insist, it is not optional. It is a command of God; therefore a man who decides to become a Promise Keeper embraces sexual purity and all that it demands. Jerry Kirk, president of the National Coalition Against Pornography, writes in one of the books published under the auspices of Promise Keepers:

> For the single man, this means a willingness to wait until marriage for sexual intercourse. God's call to virginity before marriage is unequivocal. For those who have made a mistake already, it means making a commitment today to a "secondary virginity" that will wait for your spouse . . . Purity also means obeying Jesus' command not to lust after that which is not ours (See Matt. 5:27–28). This is tough! It means not putting ourselves in a position to use women sexually either by thought or by action (e.g., pornography is an exploitive form of mental intercourse). For the single man, it means treating every woman he dates in a manner that respects and preserves her purity for her future husband. Purity also means seeking to follow Christ's call in spirit, not just by the letter of the law. It does *not* mean trying to find a thin line marking the boundary of what's acceptable and crawling right up to the edge (and maybe even peering over a few times).
>
> For us married men, sexual purity means reflecting God's absolute faithfulness to us in our faithfulness to our wives. Adultery can take many forms. Watching racy movies on a business trip in an airport hotel, with or without masturbation, is a form of emotional adultery that will eventually weaken the marriage.[4]

Promise Keepers acknowledge that, in the past, Christian men and non-Christian men have been almost indistinguishable in regard to their personal morality. Statistics on divorce, extramarital affairs, child abuse, addictions to pornography, and domestic violence are almost identical for those men who attend church regularly as those who do not. Here again, Promise Keepers has noted the correlation between the lack of accountability and the preponderance of sexual misconduct among Christian men. To the Promise Keepers at Boulder, John Maxwell cited research done by seminary professor Howard Hendricks: "In a survey he took of over five hundred men who had fallen sexually, he said there were three things that he found out about those men that were consistent. Number one, they had no time alone with God. They weren't spending the time with God that they needed to. Number two, there was no accountability. They had nobody to whom they were accountable. Number three, they said they never thought that it could happen to them."[5]

Promise Keepers hopes to change those statistics as men commit themselves to maintaining spiritual, moral, ethical, and sexual purity.

PROMISE FOUR

> *A Promise Keeper is committed to building strong marriages and families through love, protection, and biblical values.*

While some observers are fond of referring to Promise Keepers as "muscular Christianity," the movement has a tender side as well, especially when it comes to building marriages and families. Whether a Promise Keeper is married or not, he is expected to honor women in general, hold a high view of marriage and motherhood, and support the structure of the traditional two-parent family.

The married Promise Keeper is expected to love his wife, to honor her, care for her. But he is not to stop with mere sentiment.

Promise Keepers talk a lot about honoring others: God, children, pastors, and especially wives. Perhaps nobody talks about this kind of honor more than the author of numerous bestselling books and videos, Gary Smalley. Smalley may be best known for his television infomercials on how to improve a marriage, featuring celebrities such as Dick Clark, John Tesh, and Frank and Kathie Lee Gifford. At the 1995 Denver PK conference, Smalley told how honoring his wife had come to be such an important part of his life message. Smalley had been married only five years when one day he came home from work and his wife refused to talk to him.

"What's wrong?" Gary asked.

"Nothing," his wife responded coldly.

Smalley recognized that something significant was going on, so he continued to talk with his wife. At one point, he asked, "What do you think is the key to us being so unhappy and causing us to go downhill so rapidly?"

Smalley's wife responded, "I feel that you treat everyone and everything on this earth as more valuable than you treat me."

"Explain that to me," Gary shot back.

"When you come home, you watch TV, or you will go off to the garage to work on one of your projects, or on the weekend you will go off with the guys. I feel like I don't even exist! And I have been looking forward to spending time with you, or I will prepare a really neat meal, then someone will call and you will say, 'Oh, I'm not doing anything important,' and you're off."

That day, Smalley asked his wife if she would forgive him for the way he had been treating her for the first five years of their marriage. Then Gary made a commitment that transformed his marriage. He said, "From this day forward, for the rest of my life, I want you to be the most important human being on this earth." Smalley began to honor his wife in this manner, trying on a daily basis to make her feel like, to him, she was the most important person on earth.

Gary Smalley told the crowd at Denver, "That [commitment] has changed our life . . . we've now been married for over thirty years and I still see [honoring] as the basis of our marriage."[6]

As a corollary to honoring his wife, a Promise Keeper is also to show his love for her by serving her. It is this aspect of Promise Keepers that is so enigmatic to those who do not understand the biblical basis upon which the organization operates. At the same time Promise Keepers teaches that husbands and wives must submit to each other (Ephesians 5:20), it also advocates the position that the husband-father should be the head of the household, that the man should be the family leader. The essence of the Promise Keeper's leadership, however, is not dictatorial, but rather is earned through serving his wife and children.

Some of the movement's critics have accused Promise Keepers of being misogynist, teaching men to dominate and manipulate women. Any concept can be abused, of course, but in fact Promise Keepers teaches husbands to surrender their egos to serve their wives.

Bob Blume, Promise Keepers' senior event manager, is the man in charge of all the logistical details involved in preparing a stadium for a Promise Keepers conference. Bob tells a story about his friend Paul Barr, whose Detroit-area construction company donated the services of a huge scissors-lift to hoist Promise Keepers' main television cameras in the center of the field at the 1995 Promise Keepers conference in the Pontiac

Silverdome. The conference was about to begin, and for some reason the scissors-lift was not working.

Bob Blume called Paul Barr at his office and said, "Paul, please come to the stadium right away. We're having a problem with your scissors-lift."

By the time Barr walked into the Pontiac Silverdome, the stadium was packed with 72,000 men, roaring, "We love Jesus, yes we do. We love Jesus, how 'bout you?"

Barr looked around in awe, and all he could say was, "Wow!"

"The scissors-lift, Paul!" Bob Blume urged him.

Barr could not take his eyes off the men in the stadium.

"Paul!" Blume nudged him to get his attention. "The scissors-lift!"

"Huh? Oh, yeah. Where did you say it is supposed to be?"

"It's going to be right in the middle of the stadium. It has to hold our television cameras."

Paul quickly went to work on repairing a minor malfunction in the scissors-lift, positioned the television cameras, and returned to where Bob Blume was standing, in the stadium tunnel leading to the locker room. Still awestruck at seeing so many men gathered to worship God, Barr asked, "Do you mind if I stay?"

"Of course not," replied Bob Blume. "I'll get you a seat."

Paul Barr stayed throughout the entire Detroit conference. At the close of the meetings on Saturday, Bob Blume asked Paul how he had been affected by the conference and what difference it was going to make in his marriage. "I don't know," Barr replied, "but I can tell you one thing. If I know my wife, she is going to try to out-serve me, and it isn't going to happen!"

On Saturday night, Paul Barr got home late, but as he slipped into bed, he said to his wife, "The man who crawls into bed with you tonight will not be the same man who gets out of this bed tomorrow morning." With that, Paul closed his eyes and fell fast asleep.

The following morning, Paul's wife called him for breakfast. Paul went downstairs and sat down at the breakfast table, and just sat there.

"Hurry up and eat your breakfast," his wife said. "It's going to get cold."

"No, I'm waiting for you," he replied.

"What do you mean, you're waiting for me?"

"I'm waiting to pray with you."

It was the first time in their marriage that they had ever prayed together at the breakfast table. Following breakfast, Paul went upstairs to take a shower. While he was in the shower, he heard his wife call, "Paul, I just set your lunch beside the door. I'll see you later." And she left.

With the water splashing over his body, Paul Barr suddenly realized that it had been thirteen years since his wife had last packed his lunch for him.

Paul hopped out of the shower, his body naked and still dripping wet, and went over and made the bed. It was the first time in the nineteen years of their marriage that Paul had ever made the bed. It was the beginning of a transformation in Paul Barr's life and in his marriage. He and his wife have been trying to out-serve each other ever since!

Besides its emphasis upon the husband and wife relationship, Promise Keepers is committed to helping men be better fathers to their children. Many men have been so busy trying to give their children a better life that they miss out on giving their kids the one thing the children want and need more than anything—Dad. Other men have dropped out of the family photographs by default, and desperately need to adjust their priorities to get back into the center of the family. Psychologist Gary Rosberg was such a fellow.

While speaking at the 1996 Indianapolis Promise Keepers conference, Rosberg showed the men a picture his daughter Sarah had drawn of their family during the time he was cramming for his doctoral thesis in counseling several years earlier. At first Rosberg had tried to placate his daughter by saying, "Ahh, that's nice. I'll hang it on the dining room wall."

After Sarah left the room, Gary refocused his attention on his studies. But something about his daughter's drawing gnawed at him. Looking again at Sarah's stick figures, Rosberg suddenly realized what was wrong. There was Mommy; Sarah; sister Missy; the dog Katie . . . but one person was missing. *Where's Dad?* Rosberg reeled in grief as he understood that there was no dad in his daughter's picture of their family.

Gary Rosberg called Sarah back into the room. Pointing at her picture, he asked gently, "Honey, where's your daddy?"

"Oh, you're at the library," Sarah answered innocently.

The weight of Sarah's statement hit Gary Rosberg like a Mack truck. To his abject despair, he realized that in the eleven-year process of working toward his doctor's degree, while keeping a full-time job, he had squandered away his relationship with his family. He had been at the library.

In the ensuing weeks, Gary Rosberg became Dr. Gary Rosberg, psychologist and professional family counselor. What's wrong with this picture?

One evening, Rosberg forced himself to bring up the subject with his wife, Barbara. Speaking tentatively, Gary asked, "Barbara, is it too late for me to come home?"

Rosberg's wife knew what he meant, but for a long moment she said nothing. Finally she responded, "The girls and

I love you very much. We want you home, but you haven't been here. I've felt like a single parent for years."

Gary Rosberg—Dr. Gary Rosberg—recognized that he had become a stranger in his own home. Over the next few days, he determined what he had to do. He would attempt to win his family back, regardless of the cost. He knew he could not demand their love and respect. He had to earn it by serving his wife and children.

In retrospect, Rosberg said, "I had put up a veneer. I had blocked my family out. Nothing could get through. It took the naïveté of a little girl to break through the wall that eleven years of college and a full-time job had built around my heart."

Rosberg took seriously the task of winning back his family. The first step was to seek help from the small group of men with whom he met regularly. Even there, Rosberg found that he had to humbly admit he had been a fraud. For years he had been presenting himself to the group as having it all together. Now, he asked the fellows to forgive him for his pride and superficiality. He told the group, "I'm hurting and I need your help to restore my family."

As Rosberg sought to change his priorities, he recalled his own father's commitment to honoring his mother by spending the first hour after work at home with her, giving her his undivided attention. Gary began doing something similar with Barbara, making time with her a priority.

Similarly, he made special efforts to reconnect with his two daughters. "Every four to six weeks I ask Sarah, 'How am I doing? What do you need more of from me?' 'Missy, what do you need less of from me?' And it's always the same. They want my time and attention. They're not impressed that I speak at conventions or write a book. All they know is, I'm not at their basketball game, or I wasn't there to pick up the pizza."

One day, several months after Gary had begun the restoration process, Sarah bounded into his office with a new picture she had drawn. As Gary Rosberg looked at the picture, he knew he was making progress. There in Sarah's stick drawing was Missy, and Barb, Kitty the dog, Sarah . . . yes! There was Dad right in the center of the picture.

Rosberg says, "I went out and bragged to my guys and told them, 'There's a new picture, and Sarah put me in it.' That picture stays on the wall of my office, so I can always see it."[7]

The fourth promise is designed to help men see their families as their number one priority after God, and to encourage them to get back into the center of their family's picture.

Promises Five, Six, and Seven are intended to widen the Promise Keeper's lens.

CHAPTER 5

TAKING IT TO THE STREETS

In recent years, it has been unpopular to speak well of churches and other religious organizations, and especially of pastors or priests. In polls surveying the level of respect people have for men in various occupations, men in the ministry frequently land near the bottom, usually right above (and sometimes below) used car dealers, insurance salesmen, and ambulance-chasing accident lawyers. Part of the disrespect shown to churches and clerics must be attributed to the widely publicized ministerial scandals of the late 1980s and early 1990s. Whereas pastors and priests previously ranked at the top of surveys listing the most trusted men in the world, and the Elmer Gantry–type of preacher made for sleazy fiction fodder, now it is assumed by the public that most ministers are of Elmer's ilk until proven otherwise. As a result, many noble churches and dedicated pastors and priests have been denigrated and generally unappreciated.

Not surprisingly, this dearth of respect has decimated churches and ministerial ranks. Many churches are relatively empty; an ever-shrinking percentage of people attend church services regularly nowadays. A survey done by the Luntz Research polling firm, reported in *George* magazine, found that 86 percent of Americans believe in God.[1] Yet, according to religion pollster George Barna, only 42 percent of Americans claim to be churchgoers, a decline from 49 percent in 1986.[2] Of the "baby busters," the generation born between 1965 and 1983, only 33 percent attend weekly church services.[3] Fewer and fewer men are entering the ministry; in the Catholic church, for example, the shortage of priests has been at crisis level for some time.

Exacerbating the problem, discouraged pastors are quitting in record numbers. In one major denomination in the United States, an average of two pastors are resigning every day. Pastoral surveys consistently report that nearly 80 percent of those pastors who remain on the job have seriously considered quitting within the past three months of the poll. Many pastors have had their marriages shredded by the ministry. The president of one of the largest denominations in America confided recently that his group is losing 125 pastors per month to divorce.

Historically, when the mainstream church has flagged, one of the quickest ways for an individual or group to rise to prominence among spiritually minded people has been to rail against the inadequacies and failures of the church and its leaders. One of the most intriguing paradoxes of Promise Keepers is that it does the exact opposite. Against an overwhelming tide of public opinion, Promise Keepers honors the church and its leaders.

PROMISE FIVE

> *A Promise Keeper is committed to supporting the mission of his church by honoring and praying for his pastor, and by actively giving his time and resources.*

Does that mean Promise Keepers is a church, or planning to become a new denomination? On the contrary, Promise Keepers makes a concerted effort to funnel men back to their local congregation, even if that particular body may not be in complete agreement with Promise Keepers' theological positions. "We are not, have never been, and never will be a church or a denomination," a PK executive told me straightforwardly.

Interestingly, you can't really join Promise Keepers. The closest Promise Keepers comes to soliciting new "members" is near the close of the weekend stadium conferences, when men are invited to become "Committed Promise Keepers." The men do so simply by filling out a brief commitment card and dropping it in a bucket for "offerings" (financial gifts)—PK does receive one offering at each conference in addition to the registration fees—or by sending it directly to PK headquarters in Denver. In return, Committed Promise Keepers are sent a certificate signifying that they have taken their stand. They also receive a personalized commitment card.

By accepting the label of a Committed Promise Keeper, the men are indicating that they agree with the Promise Keepers statement of faith enclosed in the conference syllabus. The Committed Promise Keeper also concurs with the Seven Promises of a Promise Keeper, also included in the syllabus. Promise Keepers literature makes it clear that men who sign the commitment cards and return them to PK are not so much joining an organization as an *organism*, a living, breathing group of men who have chosen to become known as "men of integrity."

In every Promise Keepers syllabus, right next to the commitment card, is a page explaining, "Becoming a Committed Promise Keeper is . . . about making a daily decision to walk out your promises . . . in the context of the local church." Promise Keepers consistently points men back to their local churches.

Bob Blume, who facilitates the huge Promise Keepers stadium conferences, believes that the organization's best efforts are insufficient without the local church. Says Blume, "If we just do stadium conferences, we really haven't accomplished much. It's similar to going to hear outstanding motivational speakers. It's worth doing; it's extremely inspiring, and you come away from the event really juiced up, but most of what you hear will not stay with you long-term. That's why our goal is to have the guys go back home and get involved in a men's ministry in a local church. That way they can take what they have heard, apply it in their lives, and put down some roots in the church and the community where it will truly make a difference."

Promise Keepers purports that it is a catalyst for the local church, not a detriment to it. Even the scheduling of Promise Keepers events is designed to cooperate with the majority of churches. All stadium conferences, for instance, conclude early on Saturday evening, allowing the men in attendance plenty of time to get back home for services at their home churches on Sunday morning. Indeed, in many cases the men can hardly wait to return to their home congregations to transplant some of the enthusiasm they experienced at the PK rally.

*   *   *

Promise Keepers seem to have a special place in their hearts for pastors. Recognizing that many pastors are hurting, weary, struggling with feelings of discouragement and meaninglessness, and have no one with whom they can safely share their burdens, PK makes a special effort to affirm pastors who attend the stadium conferences. The practice of inviting the pastors to the front of the stadium stage to receive affirmation and to be prayed for has become a highlight of Promise Keepers events ever since it began, at the 1993 Boulder conference. While pastors—from the most unassuming to the most ostentatious—file to the front, the men in the stadium erupt in a thunderous roar, standing to their feet, applauding and cheering wildly. Many of the pastors are overworked, underpaid, and starving for an encouraging word, but if anyone knows how to pump up a group of men to spur them on, it is McCartney and company.

"They need it," roars McCartney into the microphone. "They all need it! They need us to hug them, to embrace them, and to be with them." The men bellow back their approval. Tears flow freely as pastors bask in the accolades they never anticipated receiving this side of the pearly gates.

Some pastors and laymen, however, feel that Promise Keepers' attitude is condescending toward clergymen. Said one Missouri minister, "All this cheerleading and talk of how weary and wounded I am makes me feel like a warped weirdo who cannot handle my own problems. Sure, I have troubles, and yes, I carry the extra load of my congregation's needs, but I'm not some needy, perverted, incompetent, bumbling oaf who needs the cheers and support of other people to function. I can make it on my own, thank you."

Most pastors, however, are extremely grateful for Promise Keepers' emphasis upon honoring pastors. The vast majority of pastors welcome and appreciate the men who have prayed for them at the stadium conferences. Frequently, the prayer for the pastors at the large rally is a preview to what happens when the men go home. A young pastor attending the PK conference in Boise burst into tears as a group of men from his church placed their hands on his shoulders and prayed for him and his family. Later the pastor revealed, "I had been ready to quit the ministry and had only accompanied the men to the conference because I had paid my registration fee and didn't want to waste the money. I had planned to resign my pastoral position at our church's next governing board meeting the following week.

"But the Promise Keepers affirmation gave me a second wind. Because of the conference, the men of my congregation realized that they had been taking me for granted. Prior to attending the Promise Keepers event at Boise, several of the older men had frequently criticized my youthful enthusiasm and were quick to point out my many mistakes and failures."

The men confessed their error, asked God and the young pastor to forgive them, and pledged to meet every Saturday morning to do nothing else but pray for their pastor. That young man has remained in the ministry at the same church, his faith and effectiveness increased.

As a result of their attendance at Promise Keepers, the men in his church have become much more involved in the ministry and in the community. They realize that they were remiss for not actively supporting their church. They are now helping the pastor do many of the ministry functions, such as visiting hospitalized and shut-in members of the church, counseling couples who are planning to get married, and taking care of many of the church administrative matters that had previously landed on the pastor's desk. Beyond that, several of the men have begun supporting the church financially— something Promise Keepers encourages the men to do before giving to any other charitable group, including PK. The men from the young pastor's church started giving 10 percent and more of their income toward the local church budget, something they had not done before attending the PK conference.

"I think I can honestly say that, had it not been for that Promise Keepers conference and the impact it has had upon our church's men, I would probably be in some form of secular employment today," the pastor said. "But thanks to the love and affirmation I received there, and the fact that it has continued to this day, not only do I still have a ministry, but our church will never be the same."

Sensing that pastors needed a conference of their own, Promise Keepers decided to hold a special men's clergy event in February 1996 at the Georgia Dome in Atlanta. Promise Keepers was so convinced the pastors should convene that it provided more than $1.6 million in scholarships and financial aid for pastors whose churches could not or would not pay their way.[4] More than 39,000 pastors showed up at the unprecedented gathering, men from a wide spectrum of denominational backgrounds, from Southern Baptists to Pentecostals to Catholics. They came from nearly every state and nation in North and South America. Pastors representing more than seventy Native American tribes were on hand, as were inner-city pastors, "uptown" pastors, rural and suburban pastors, and even a scruffy-looking contingency of "biker-pastors."

For three days, the men heard uplifting messages of encouragement. They also heard hard-hitting messages on the need to repent of their past prejudices, pride, ambition, and animosity toward other churches, pastors, and racial groups. On the final evening of the conference, the pastors confessed their own sins to each other and to God, asking for forgiveness. Despite their differences, they pledged to work together in unity to help break down walls of resentment in the world by modeling God's love. To formalize their intent, a representative group of pastors signed a document known as "The Atlanta Covenant."

The document is basically an expansion of the Seven Promises into a prayer, but with an interesting twist. The pastors began not by pledging to keep the promises, but by admitting that they have broken them. Addressing themselves to God, they wrote, "We acknowledge, confess and repent before You that although we may not be guilty of all that is stated below, we are prompted by godly sorrow to repent because we as clergy have sinned against You (1 Cor. 7:10–11). Therefore, we enter into this 'Atlanta Covenant' with You and with each other."[5] The clergymen then went on to describe areas relating to each of the Seven Promises in which they had been negligent, wrong, or sinful. Where those errors existed, they committed themselves to constructive change in the future. For example, relating to Promise Three, the pastors pledged, "Where we have excused our moral and sexual sin and have been neither repentant nor broken, we now offer our bodies to You as living sacrifices. We ask that You transform our minds and hearts by Your Word and Your Holy Spirit."[6]

The clergy conference focused attention on two issues that, for all the Promise Keepers' flowery rhetoric, continue to separate a large majority of Christians—racial prejudice and denominational friction. Promise Keepers declared 1996 as the year to "Break Down the Walls." The issue, however, was not new for PK. Although it has only recently surged to the forefront as a signature message of Promise Keepers, it was one of the original Seven Promises.

PROMISE SIX

> *A Promise Keeper is committed to reaching beyond any racial and denominational barriers to demonstrate the power of biblical unity.*

While the leadership of Promise Keepers may be somewhat idealistic, they are not naive. They know they must be willing to start small. At most public conferences, every Promise Keeper is encouraged to begin the process of racial reconciliation by establishing a bona fide, ongoing relationship with one person from a racial background disparate from his own. That is a stretch for the many Promise Keepers who prefer the preponderance of white faces surrounding them at the stadium events. But PK is making an impact in racial reconciliation. Symbolically, at least, Promise Keepers may be building stronger and more lasting bridges of racial reconciliation than any other movement in America—religious or otherwise. In addition to Coach Bill McCartney's repeated messages on the issue of racism, many other PK speakers have shocked the largely white, Anglo-Saxon, Protestant elements in the stands by their statements and actions.

For example, in April 1995 at the Detroit PK conference, in front of 72,280 men, Promise Keepers president Randy Phillips—a fair-haired white man—and Wellington Boone, an African American pastor from Richmond who often carries the PK torch of racial reconciliation and was one of the speakers on the PK program, stood face-to-face on the stage. They confessed their racial sins to each other and sought forgiveness, all with the microphones on for everyone to hear.

The following year at the clergy conference in Atlanta,

Boone did something even more radical. In a spontaneous, unplanned move, Boone suddenly announced during his speech, "There's something that has never been confessed at these [Promise Keepers] gatherings—the sin perpetrated against black men by black men." Boone then addressed Dr. Tony Evans, the popular African American pastor from Dallas, who has been severely criticized by other black leaders for his willingness to cooperate with "white" Christianity. Facing Evans, Wellington Boone said, "You have absorbed a lot of criticism by your own brothers for standing with Promise Keepers, but I want to affirm that you are a man of God. If I had some water right now, I would wash your feet."

Someone brought a basin of water onto the stage, and Boone held true to his words. Following Jesus' example of washing his disciples' feet as a gesture of humility (recorded in the New Testament's Gospel of John), Boone proceeded to kneel down in front of Evans. The other preacher removed his shoes and socks and covered his face with his hands while Wellington Boone washed his feet in front of more than 42,000 other pastors.

Staged? Grandiose? Showboating? Perhaps. But Tony Evans later said, "No greater honor has ever been bestowed on me than this."

Bill McCartney himself is probably the loudest voice among Promise Keepers calling for racial reconciliation. At the 1996 Pittsburgh conference, McCartney bluntly hammered home his message: "There is a spirit of white racial superiority that exists in our land. It is defined as an insensitivity to the pain of people of color. We do not know their pain." The mostly white crowd applauded wildly. Whether the Promise Keepers will actually do anything more than clap their hands in favor of racial reconciliation remains to be seen, but Promise Keepers' courage to include Promise Six is laudable.

Less controversial, though equally daunting, is Promise
Keepers' obsession with breaking down the walls between
Christian denominations. Speakers at Promise Keepers
events are fond of emphasizing the commonalities of faith,
things all Christians have in common and can agree on, indeed things that most of the world's major religions can agree
upon. Near the conclusion of one Promise Keepers event, I
looked across the press box at a reporter who made no secret
of the fact that he is a socialist-leaning, atheistic secular humanist. Interested in knowing his first impressions of PK, I
nodded to the men who were standing and singing during a
break in the speaking. "What do you think?" I asked.

He shrugged his shoulders and replied, "What's not to like?
Love your wife, take care of your kids, find some friends you
can be honest with, be nice to people—even those you don't
know anything about. Who can argue with that?"

Acknowledging that many fellow Christians of differing
denominational affiliations are not always amicable, premier
Christian author Max Lucado spoke directly to the issue of
Christian unity at the 1996 Clergy Conference in Atlanta. Putting a new twist on an oft-used metaphor, Lucado compared
Christianity to a stately ship with Jesus as the captain. But
according to Lucado, it is a rocky boat:

> There is trouble on deck. Fights have broken out be-
> tween sailors. There have been times—incredibly as it
> may seem—when one group even refused to acknowl-
> edge the presence of any other group on the ship! Most
> tragically, some adrift at sea have chosen not to board
> this boat. "Life is choppy on the ocean," they say, "fac-
> ing the waves and the elements, but I'd rather face the
> waves," they say, "than to get caught in between a fight
> between two sailors."[7]

Referring to Jesus' prayer for his disciples on the night before he died on the Cross (John 17), Lucado pointed out, "On the last night of his life, our master did not pray for the health of the disciples, for the success of the disciples, even for the happiness of the disciples. He prayed that they would get along with each other." Lucado paused long enough to look around at the 39,000 pastors in attendance before declaring, "We are seeing the answer to that prayer today."

While Promise Keepers revel in their unity, espousing that their diversity enhances that unity, denominational differences do exist. And they do not always exist for picayune reasons such as one party wanting red carpet in the church while another prefers beige. Many of the differences are deeply embedded in profound theological thought and cannot be waved away with a "Let's just talk about Jesus" sweep of the hand. Nor does it seem realistic to assume, as Promise Keepers does, that all Christians can worship effectively in the charismatic-flavored style propagated without explanation or apology by Promise Keepers' singers and musicians.

One pastor of a Lutheran church told me that he would not be attending Promise Keepers himself, nor would he recommend it to the men in his congregation. "I went to the first large Promise Keepers convocation nearby," he explained. "I did not relish the idea of going, but several leading men in our church wanted to attend, and insisted that I accompany them. Reluctantly, I went. I was impressed by the magnitude of the conference, but from the moment it began, I felt uncomfortable and out of place. I was not accustomed to the loud music. While we Lutherans consider ourselves enthusiastic singers, we much prefer the rich, melodious sounds of a pipe organ to drums, guitars, and synthesizers.

"The Promise Keepers concept of praise and worship had distinctly charismatic elements—men raising their hands, praying aloud, in a noisy, jumbled mass. Several men near me were jumping up and down as part of their expressions of praise. Others locked arms and were kicking up their feet and legs as though they were a dance troupe performing to the music. Many were speaking in tongues, while others simply shouted, hooted, whistled, and roared as loudly as possible. The sound was so overpowering, I could not think clearly enough to articulate my prayers.

"While I appreciated the Promise Keepers' enthusiasm, our Lutheran form of worship is much quieter, more liturgical, more introspective, and frankly, I am fond of that. We do not talk a great deal in our church about 'being born again' or 'breaking down walls.' We like our walls right where they are."

Similar to that Lutheran pastor, many other church leaders do not want to see their denominational distinctions blurred by Promise Keepers or anyone else. We'll take a closer look at some of the opposition to Promise Keepers by Christian denominations in a later chapter. Regardless of the opposition, however, it is refreshing to find, in Promise Keepers, a group of Christians who do not see other Christians, or even other religions, as the enemy.

The final promise brings us full circle, back to Jesus and his "Great Commandment" to love God and to love one another; and his "Great Commission" to go to all the nations in the world and make disciples everywhere.

PROMISE SEVEN

> *A Promise Keeper is committed to influencing his world, being obedient to the Great Commandment (see Mark 12:30–31) and the Great Commission (see Matt. 28:19–20).*

The Great Commandment according to Promise Keepers is Jesus' instruction to love God with all your being, and to love your neighbor as yourself. The actions and attitudes of all true Promise Keepers are supposed to be motivated by love—love for God, love for their own families, and love for humankind. But to love God supremely and to love your neighbor as yourself is easier to talk about than to do, especially when it comes to loving the unlovely, or loving people who do not look, act, think, or respond the way you do. Nevertheless, Promise Keepers is at least ostensibly committed to keep loving even those people who do not love them back.

When this sort of love is actually expressed, whether it be to a spouse who has given up on a marriage, to a child who resents a parent, or to someone of a different race or culture who has been steeped in prejudice and bitterness, it is contagious. Coach McCartney tells a story of a man who visited a leper colony. Inside the leprosarium he met many men who because of their pain and suffering had developed a resentment toward God and other people, but one man seemed to have a brighter outlook on life. The visitor approached the leper and asked, "What is it about you that makes you so different?"

The leper answered, "Well, one day, a guy came in here

and told me about Jesus Christ, telling me how much he loved me. And I spit in his face and cursed him and threw food at him and chased him away. But he came back the next day and again started telling me about Jesus and his love, and I spit in his face and cursed him and threw food at him and chased him away. Finally he came back so many times that I could no longer deny him, and I prayed and asked Jesus Christ to come into my life."

"How often did he come back before you did that?" the visitor asked.

The leper replied, "He came back every day for thirteen years."[8]

Whether Coach Mac's story is real or apocryphal, it illustrates the kind of unconditional, persevering love Promise Keepers are expected to express to the world around them. A love that will not quit, a love that will not be denied, a love that has its source and end in God.

In addition to emulating Jesus' example to love God and his creations, Promise Keepers take seriously Jesus' Great Commission, his command to his followers to take the Gospel into all the world and to make disciples. This commission instills in the movement an evangelistic fervor similar to that of many other Christian organizations, but Promise Keepers has chosen to take a different tact than simply trying to convert people on the basis of their message alone. They hope to make an impact by—of all things—modeling Christian character and conduct.

Promise Keepers base their approach on Jesus' words, "You are the light of the world . . . let your light shine before men, that they may see your good deeds and praise your Father in heaven" (Matthew 5:14–16 NIV).

The good deeds that Promise Keepers try to do go beyond maintaining fidelity to marriage vows and making children a priority. They even go beyond doing things to help out in their home church. Promise Keepers let their light shine by serving the cities—volunteering to clean, repair, and paint inner-city homes and churches. The first such project, called "Serve the City," was held in Denver and Dallas. Others followed in Washington, D.C., and Oakland, California. Promise Keepers, excited about being able to put real meaning into their pledge to uphold Promises Six and Seven, showed up ready to work in the less advantaged areas of these urban communities. The recipients of the Promise Keepers' efforts were amazed. They could hardly believe that the men would be willing to cross denominational, racial, and socioeconomic barriers and freely give of themselves in painstaking labor. But to Promise Keepers, it was simply putting their "muscular" Christianity to work.

The Seven Promises are the philosophical and practical underpinnings of Promise Keepers. Fail to understand these promises, and Promise Keepers will continue to be an enigma to you. Once you understand, however, that this new men's movement is a fresh telling of the old story of the Gospel, it is less baffling. Still, few spiritually based men's movements have survived for long, much less had the impact that Promise Keepers has had and continues to have. What are they doing differently? Why are they so successful?

A large measure of Promise Keepers' success must be attributed to the fact that, since the founding of the organization in 1990, they have not deviated from their original mission, encapsulated in their first and only mission statement: "Promise Keepers is a Christ-centered ministry dedicated to uniting men through vital relationships to become godly influences in their world."

And men by the tens of thousands are responding. But what attracted them to Promise Keepers? What did they hope to gain? One thing is certain, the keepers of the promises have some stories to tell, as we will see in the next chapter.

CHAPTER 6

THE KEEPERS OF THE PROMISES

"Hey! Put out that stinking cigar!" a man shouted as he leaned over the seat in front of him at the Oakland Coliseum.

The brawny man to whom the words were spoken slowly stood to his feet and turned around. Still holding the stogie between his teeth, he replied gruffly, "How would you like for me to put you out?" He glowered at the man who had dared confront him.

The nonsmoker did not back down. "Come on, man. I'm not looking for trouble, but this is a Promise Keepers rally. You aren't supposed to be smoking at this thing."

"I didn't see any signs saying there's no smoking."

"So what? You wouldn't smoke in church, would you?"

"I ain't in church, I'm at the Coliseum." With that, the man sat back down and continued puffing. Throughout the first speaker's message on Friday night, a conspicuous swirl of smoke could be seen rising from one section of seats, high in the Coliseum stands.

The opening speaker for that PK conference was Raul

Ries, a former Vietnam veteran who had grown up in a neighborhood even the police were reluctant to patrol. Ries learned to fend for himself and seemed to have a natural enmity within him. In Nam, Ries was assigned to a unit known as the "Bounty Hunters."

"We killed people," Ries told the audience. "I had grown up in an abusive, crime-ridden environment, and here I was in a foreign country being ordered to take people's lives without consequences. What more could a homicidal young punk ask?" Killing became too easy for Ries; after ten months in Vietnam, he was sent home and committed to a psychiatric hospital. When he got out, he was still aching for a fight. He spent most of his time drinking and doing drugs. Finally, his wife of two years couldn't take it anymore. She threatened to leave.

In a rage, Ries loaded his automatic weapons. "I was out of my mind, stomping around the house," he recalls, "when I accidentally bumped into the television. It popped on. I stood there stunned for a moment, watching some preacher named Chuck Smith from a church called Calvary Chapel. It seemed as if he was talking to me, about how sin can overtake your life. About how God loves us. It made me so furious that I almost shot the tube out."

With his finger on the trigger, Ries stood listening to the television preacher telling him how he could find forgiveness and a fresh start by trusting Jesus Christ. The preacher on the screen said that by dying on the Cross, Jesus had already paid the ultimate price for humankind's sins, and had forged a way so all people—everywhere—could now be free from the past and guaranteed a wonderful future.

Ries allowed the gun to drop to the floor as he fell to his knees, sobbing uncontrollably. There on the living room floor, God performed a miracle. Raul felt forgiven and clean on the inside. Soon he would experience freedom from his addiction to drugs, alcohol, and violence.

The first person Ries told about his conversion was his wife. He begged her forgiveness and told her he had found Jesus. She was skeptical. But she believed him enough to stay with him. They rebuilt their marriage and their lives and have now been married more than a quarter of a century. Raul went on to become an ordained minister under the auspices of—guess who?—Chuck Smith and his Calvary Chapel.[1]

As Ries told his story to 49,000 men at the Oakland Promise Keepers conference, one man, cigar smoke floating over his head like a cloud, sat in especially rapt attention. When Ries extended the invitation for men who wanted to come forward for prayer, the man with the cigar was one of the first men in the stadium to leap to his feet. He bounded down the stadium steps and didn't stop until two evangelism volunteers corralled him near the front of the stage. There the three men got on their knees and prayed.

Later the cigar smoker said, "I don't know how that speaker did it, but he keyed into several areas of my life that were about to explode: my anger at the world that I brought back with me from Vietnam, my marriage falling apart, and my addictions. I came to this conference with a buddy who bought my ticket. I figured that since I catch all the other shows when they come to Oakland, why not this one? But I never expected something like this. I am going home to my wife and I am going to ask her to forgive me and to go to church with me on Sunday. I've messed up pretty badly, but now, with God's help, I want to start clean and do it right."

Not everyone who attends a Promise Keepers event comes away transformed, of course, but many do. Todd Smith, an executive with an oil lease company, attended the Promise Keepers conference in Houston. "I knew my life was out of control long before I attended Promise Keepers," he said later. "But I was stymied by my inability to handle my priorities. I had survived the oil price crash of the eighties, but only by working my tail off. My desk perpetually overflowed with work that should have been done last week, or last month. I worked long hours, often not getting home until after my wife and children had already gone to bed. I saw them in the morning as we all scrambled to get ready for work and school, and I honestly tried to be part of their lives. I took days off sometimes just to be with them, but then I'd have to work twice as hard to catch up on the work that didn't get done while I was gone. I was in a pit and it seemed no matter which way I tried to climb out, I kept sliding farther into quicksand.

"A friend of mine who is in the same industry invited me to go to Promise Keepers with him. At first I turned him down. I didn't understand much about Promise Keepers. Most of the articles I had read about them left me cold. I wasn't interested in any men's movement. I was barely hanging on to my own life and that of my family. But my friend was quietly persistent. He was never abrasive, but he continued to ask me to go with him during the weeks preceding the conference. It wasn't Promise Keepers that attracted me; it was him. I could see that he obviously had some secret for handling the pressures of our work that I did not. I knew that he lived with the same stress that I did, yet he seemed to have a sense of peace that I would have given my next year's salary to have for even one night.

"Eventually I gave in and accepted his invitation. My wife was not real thrilled about it. After all, I was hardly spending any time at home during daylight hours as it was, and now I was going to take off a Friday night and all day Saturday to go out with a bunch of guys. If I was going to skip work to go anywhere, she wanted it to be with her. But she was glad that

I was at least getting out of the office for once, so she just shrugged her shoulders and said 'Have a nice time' as I went out the door.

"When my friend and I arrived at the Astrodome, I was immediately impressed by what I can only describe as a deep sense of peace. Although there was activity all around me, and thousands of men in the stadium, I felt as though I were all alone on an island with God. I had never really communicated with God very well, but now it seemed as though he was talking straight to my mind and conscience. I listened to speakers and tried to sing along with the music, but most of all I was hearing an inner voice that I had never before heard. It was as if God had put all the torn-up pieces of my life into a paper bag and was shaking them up and pouring them out on the ground. Then, as the weekend progressed, little by little it seemed he was putting the pieces back together, but this time with a whole new picture.

"When one of the speakers said something about church attendance not being enough, and that being a hard worker and provider was not good enough, that it was all useless without a real relationship with God, I knew he was talking about me. I knew I had never established a genuine relationship with the Lord, and I wanted to do that. I walked down to the front, and several fellows prayed with me. Nothing earth-shaking happened, at least not outwardly. No emotional outbursts, no fireworks, no outward signs, I guess. I didn't even *feel* different. But something in me knew that this was a serious commitment I was making.

"As I left the Astrodome on Saturday night, I was determined to make changes in my life. The first thing I did was wake up my wife and children on Sunday morning and tell them I wanted to attend church. Partly because of my work schedule and partly because of spiritual disinterest, we had not been attending church as a family. Occasionally my wife would go, but it had been ages since we had all been to church together. We went to church that day and I actually enjoyed it.

"On Sunday afternoon, I took the family out to dinner at one of the nicer restaurants in our town. As we had our meal, I began to tell them about my weekend. Then I began to apologize to them for not being the husband and dad I really wanted to be. My family loved me and understood that I had been under incredible pressure for several years, and they knew that the long, crazy hours I had been working were not in an effort to get rich, but simply to survive in my field of work. Nevertheless, as we talked, it became clear to me that they all felt that I had cheated them somehow. I had missed so many things, so many games, so many school activities, so much time with my wife. I promised them that afternoon that things were going to be different from now on. They stared back at me almost hopefully, too uncertain to get excited about anything. They took a wait-and-see attitude.

"The next day I went to work and asked for a conference with my boss. He and I sat down and I leveled with him. I told him things had not been good at my house, and that much of it had to do with the horrendous pressure I was under at work. I knew I was risking getting fired—after all, he was under the same pressure as I was, even more—but I laid out my plans. I told him, 'You know I work hard and I am good at what I do, but I cannot work eighty hours a week anymore. I will give you a full eight hours of my best efforts every day, but at five o'clock, I want to go home to my family and leave this job here.'

"At first he didn't respond. I wasn't sure if he was going to fire me or slug me. He did neither. After a long minute or two of absolute silence, he said, 'Okay, Todd. I know you have

given this company one-hundred-fifty percent for a long time.
What you are asking is not unreasonable. In fact, maybe more
of us need to do that same thing.'

"I went home and began to make my family my top priority. Sure, I still work like a maniac . . . while I am at work. But
when I walk out the office door, I try my best to leave it all
behind me. I go home to rest, to be restored, to spend time
with and to help encourage my wife and kids. I go to my kids'
ball games and we rarely miss church. My wife and I have
jump-started our dying relationship, and I thank God that I
am getting to know my kids before it is too late. It's been more
than a year since I attended that Promise Keepers conference.
I still get mail from them, but I am not actively involved in
PK. The church where we attend has a men's ministry that
existed long before Promise Keepers came on the scene, so I
have joined them and have many of the benefits of a Promise
Keepers–like accountability group. And although I am not active in PK like the friend who invited me, I will always be
grateful to him and to Promise Keepers for helping me see
what is really important in life."

Although the impact of Promise Keepers upon the inner lives
of men cannot be empirically measured, it does show up in
tangible ways in the moral character of many men. One fellow
who experienced a profound change in his lifestyle as a result
of attending the PK event at the Charlotte Motor Speedway in
June 1996 is Rob Stevens. Rob is a truck driver, or at least
that is his current occupation. After a stint in the military, he
found work on a construction crew in Atlanta building new
subdivisions for homes. Rob's wages couldn't cover his drinking and football gambling habits, and soon he turned to pilfer-
ing construction materials by sneaking into the work site at

night, loading his pickup truck full of wood, nails, plastic pipe, and anything else he could fit on the truck bed, and selling the stuff at cut-rate prices to competitors. One night, as Rob was about to pull out with a load of stolen materials, headlights from four police cruisers suddenly blinded his vision.

Rob stomped down on the gas pedal, slamming into one of the approaching police cars and careening off the front bumper of the black-and-white vehicle. Rob never looked back. He stood on the gas pedal and the pickup roared out of the construction site, leaving behind a trail of strewn wood, drywall, concrete mix, and nails.

The cruisers peeled out after Rob and gave chase. Within a minute they had caught up to him and were bearing in on him on both sides. Rob tried to do what he had seen in the movies—he yanked hard on the pickup's steering wheel, hoping to pull a spin and head off in the other direction. Instead, he succeeded only in flipping over the pickup and crashing into another police cruiser. Rob spent the next four years in prison.

Upon his release, he tried to go straight. He got a job with a trucking company driving an eighteen-wheeler, got married, and settled down—supposedly. Before long, however, Rob was slipping back into his old patterns, altering bills of lading, falsely listing the contents he was carrying, and selling whatever he could out the back doors. Besides that, he had developed another habit since he had started transporting goods across state lines: He frequented adult bookstores and dance clubs. Before long, he was spending four to five nights a week on the road, in a different town each night, in a cheap motel with another woman.

After such a night of debauchery in North Carolina, he was on his way home, passing through Charlotte early the next morning, when he noticed the huge crowd at the Motor Speedway. Thinking an auto race was getting ready to start, he wheeled his rig into one of the side parking areas and went in. Much to his disappointment, he quickly discovered that it was not a race but something called Promise Keepers happening at the speedway. He was not about to pay seventy dollars to get in, so he fast-talked his way past a volunteer security guard, convincing him that he was carrying an important load of perishable food and needed to take a look at the loading area before pulling in his rig. Once inside the speedway, Rob never looked back.

He had arrived just in time to hear the PK men's Saturday-morning singing and a strong message, along the lines of Promise Three, dealing with spiritual, moral, ethical, and sexual purity.

Rob later recalled, "As I listened to that guy talking, it was like a major league pitcher firing fastballs past me. Moral purity? Strike one; I wasn't even sure I had any morals left anymore. Ethical purity? Why, I hadn't even paid to get in! Strike two. Sexual purity? Ha! That was a joke, except for some reason I wasn't laughing. Strike three, you're out. The more I listened, the more I wanted to just jump back in my truck and get out of there, yet my feet felt as though they were riveted to the floor. Suddenly, I felt extremely uncomfortable. I was wearing my usual driving getup: T-shirt, jeans, and cowboy boots, but for some reason I suddenly felt as though I were completely naked. I actually looked at myself to make sure I wasn't exposed in front of all those guys.

"I didn't stay for the whole deal. When it got to around lunchtime, I took off. I wasn't going to stand in line with tens of thousands of guys for a bite to eat. I headed back to my truck, my heart pounding with every step. I pulled my rig out onto the highway and had just gone through the gears when I started crying. 'Weeping' probably would be a more accurate way to describe what I was doing, because as the tears flooded from my eyes, I could not even see the road. I knew I had to pull off onto the side before I killed somebody.

"When I got the truck stopped, I just sat there and bawled like a baby. I didn't even understand what I was crying about, except for the fact that I felt so cruddy on the inside—filthy as a human being—and with every tear it seemed I got a little cleaner. I was never much for praying, but right there, sitting along the side of the road, I said, 'God, if you are really there, and you can put up with me, I'd sure appreciate your help.' It wasn't much of a prayer, and probably not up to par with all those Promise Keepers' prayers, but I felt sure that God heard me.

"When I got home later that afternoon, I asked my wife to sit down because I needed to talk to her. I confessed to her that I had been up to my old tricks, that I had been doing dirty deals, robbing and cheating the suppliers who used our truck line. That was the easy part. Then I tried to tell her that I had been unfaithful to her. I didn't do a great job of explaining that part but she got the idea. She burst into tears, and ran from the room into our bedroom, slamming the door behind her. For a while I felt sure she was going to leave me. When she finally came out, she was still sobbing, and she said she needed to tell me something, too. That's when she told me that she was pregnant . . . and I was not the father.

"At first I was furious, but then I realized that I had no right whatsoever to be self-righteous when I had been so immoral myself. My wife and I talked a long time that night. We both asked each other for forgiveness and we pledged to try to make our marriage work again. The next morning, we went to church for the first time in our marriage. We didn't even know how to pick a church. We just chose one out of the newspaper listings.

"When we walked in, the first thing we saw on a bulletin board was a poster advertising the Promise Keepers event I had witnessed in Charlotte. I knew we had come to the right place."

Even men who by most standards would be called good, ethical, upstanding citizens leave Promise Keepers hoping to be better husbands, fathers, and churchmen. Perhaps most impressive is the way a Promise Keepers event affects guys who are not hooked on drugs, running around on their wives, or hostile to men of other races.

Nadine, a mother of two sons in their mid-twenties, believes Promise Keepers helped restore the relationship between her husband and their sons. "We were all together in a family business until a few years ago, when the boys and their dad got into a huge argument over something silly. One thing led to another, and before we knew it, the boys were lashing out at each other and at their dad for always caring more about the business than he did them, even as children. It got real ugly and the boys quit the business. Things became strained in the family. My husband barely talked to the boys, and our sons refused to come home except on holidays, and then for only a few hours.

"I am not even sure how it happened, but somehow all three of them attended separate Promise Keepers events. Last Thanksgiving, the boys came home, and before we began our family tradition of going around the table and each family member telling something we are thankful for, one of the boys looked straight at my husband and said, 'Before we do anything else, I want to apologize to Dad for what has happened in our family over the past year.' His brother seconded his statement.

"That opened up a whole different sort of Thanksgiving for us. My husband said, 'Oh, it was all my fault. You guys were right. I was never really there for you when you were growing up. I was always so busy trying to make the family business a success. All I wanted was to build something for you guys to take over someday. Now I see that while I was building my business, I was losing my boys. I am sorry. I know I cannot make it all up to you, but I'm willing to try.'

"My sons confessed their bitterness toward my husband and toward each other, and they and their dad were reunited that day. We were so overwhelmed with emotion—a rarity in our family—that we couldn't even eat until much later that day. Cold turkey never tasted better!"

Although the majority of men affected by Promise Keepers are white baby boomers or baby busters, older men, including men of color, are not immune to PK's contagious influence. Clarence White, a black man in his mid-sixties, who worked for twenty years on the assembly line in a General Motors automobile factory, was such a man. After his retirement in 1993, Clarence felt bored, useless, and deeply depressed. His wife, Jessie, tried to console him and encouraged him to become active in their church, but Clarence refused all of her suggestions. He spent most of his days working on an old car in their backyard, and most of his nights glued to the television set until he fell asleep.

By 1996, Clarence and Jessie's marriage was in limbo, a peaceful coexistence, neither hostile nor loving. Married for thirty-two years, they rarely argued with each other, but on the other hand, they hardly talked enough to disagree and they had not been sexually intimate in more than fifteen years. For the past several years, they had been sleeping in separate bedrooms. Feeling too old to divorce and too financially strapped to leave Clarence, Jessie resigned herself to living with him in a sort of polite, cordial, platonic relationship. In her heart, the marriage was dead, and she could only hope that either Clarence or she would also die soon.

In February 1996, a man presented some information about Promise Keepers during a Sunday morning service at Clarence and Jessie's church. Jessie was intrigued by the idea of a Christian men's movement. As the speaker told how his life had been changed by attending a PK conference in 1994, Jessie couldn't help wondering how Clarence might respond to such a gathering. *If only I could get him to go*, she thought. Clarence, however, slept through most of the presentation. He showed no interest at all in attending the event on May 10 and 11, which the PK point man had said was to take place at the Pontiac Silverdome.

Undaunted, Jessie wrote down the dates and registration details on the back of her church bulletin and placed it in her purse. Over the next ten weeks, Jessie repeatedly reminded Clarence of the approaching conference dates. She pestered him to register before it was too late. Finally, Clarence relented and dialed Promise Keepers' toll-free registration number. To Jessie's chagrin and Clarence's relief, he learned that the Detroit conference was sold out.

On May 9, late in the afternoon, one of Clarence's former shop buddies saw Clarence in his backyard tinkering with his car, so the friend stopped by to talk. During their conversation, the man said, "Clarence, several of the old boys from the shop have been planning to go to the men's meeting over at the Silverdome tomorrow and Saturday. One of the guys had to cancel because his wife is sick. Would you be interested in going along?"

Clarence's first reaction was to say no, but before he could speak, the man continued, "The ticket is already paid for. All you have to do is to show up. If you don't like it, you can leave."

Clarence reconsidered. He was tired of watching television anyhow, so this stadium conference might be a welcome diversion. "Sure, I'll go," he told his buddy.

The next day at the Silverdome, Clarence gawked in unabashed amazement. He had been to the stadium for a football game once before, several years earlier, but he could never have imagined more than seventy thousand men filling the place to talk about God. Clarence listened intently to the Friday night speakers and he was impressed by their sincerity. He found himself laughing along with the other men at some of the speakers' humorous stories, and even tapping his foot to some of the loud music.

When Clarence arrived home late Friday night, Jessie met him at the door. "How was it?" she wanted to know.

"Not bad," Clarence replied. "I guess I'll go back tomorrow. Good night." He went to his bedroom. Disappointed that Clarence seemed so unenthusiastic about the conference, Jessie retired to her bedroom.

The next morning, Clarence was up at 6:00 A.M. to make the drive from his home to the Silverdome. He didn't want to miss a minute of the conference, but he never let on to Jessie.

All day long, Clarence soaked in the messages he heard from the speakers. One fellow's words really seared into his heart. Clarence thought the speaker's name was McCartney, but he couldn't quite make it out. The man openly confessed that his marriage had been a sham for years, that he and his wife had been merely living under the same roof . . . until recently.

Clarence squirmed uncomfortably in his seat as the man spoke, but he did not leave the stadium. He listened to every word. When the man told of how he had asked his wife to forgive him, and to give him another chance, Clarence felt tears in his eyes for the first time in ages.

Clarence did not respond to any of the Promise Keepers' public invitations that weekend, but as he drove home by himself he prayed aloud, "God, you know I'm a stubborn old goat, and I've wasted a lot of years. But if you'll help me, I'll try to make whatever time you give me count. I know it sounds almost silly, but I'd be most grateful if you would help Jessie and me start over."

That night, when Clarence got home, Jessie had already gone to bed, even though it was much earlier than he had come in the night before. She just hadn't seen any reason to wait up.

Clarence turned out the porch lights and started toward his bedroom. He put on his pajamas and was about to climb into bed when he decided against it. He walked out of the bedroom toward Jessie's room. Quietly, he tiptoed inside and slowly slid beneath the covers next to his wife. Jessie did not move.

For a moment, Clarence lay still, staring toward the ceiling in the darkness. He listened carefully for sounds of Jessie's breathing, but he couldn't hear a thing. It was the first time he had been in bed this close to his wife in many years and now he wasn't even sure she was alive!

Then, suddenly, Clarence felt Jessie's hand touch his. She moved slightly toward him and whispered, "Clarence, are you all right?"

Clarence's throat had never felt as parched as it did just then, but he knew he had to speak. "Jessie, something happened to me this weekend. I'm not sure I understand it or even that I can describe it. All I know is that my heart was stirred like never before. And if you will give me a chance, and it's not too late, I'd like us to spend the rest of our lives as a married couple, not just two friends who happen to live together."

Jessie squeezed Clarence's hand tightly, as she replied, "Welcome home, Clarence."

* * *

Clearly, Promise Keepers is affecting far more men than merely those looking for a momentary spiritual high. With Promise Keepers having such a meaningful impact upon so many men, who wouldn't want to attend a conference and become a "man of integrity"?

Well, most guys, actually.

After all, why would men want to shell out their hard-earned money to go to a stadium and listen to one speaker after another remind them that they have been inadequate husbands and fathers? Moreover, how many would list establishing close relationships with other men as a burning priority? Nor do they care to get involved in overcoming racial prejudice, even if they recognize racial tension as a serious problem. In short, most guys do not care a lick about the Promise Keepers or their Seven Promises.

Other men are hesitant to attend Promise Keepers functions because they fear being asked to be open and vulnerable . . . especially in front of other men. They do not want to admit their failures. They have an image they want to protect at all costs, even though they may know that their families are falling apart right in front of them and they feel helpless to do anything about it. Other men are uncomfortable with the mass approach to dealing with intimate spiritual matters.

Still other men are not interested in Promise Keepers because they are already doing many of the things Promise Keepers encourages. Don Harper is a small businessman, married for twenty years to the same woman and father of four children. When asked to attend a Promise Keepers conference, he countered, "What for? I've been doing those things for years. I don't need a pep rally to tell me to be faithful to my wife, or to take time to be a parent to the children I helped bring into the world. Most of the guys in my church who are so cranked up about Promise Keepers are the ones who *haven't* been good husbands and fathers. They haven't been involved in the community. I'm really glad some of those guys are getting things together, but don't come bugging me about how I need to be a Promise Keeper. I *have* been a promise keeper for years. Where have you been?"

Unfortunately, for every Don Harper there are plenty of men who do need the reminders that Promise Keepers provides. Besides, few men set out to be lousy husbands and fathers. But until recently, there have been relatively few books or classes for men to help them learn the most complex job of all—being a good husband and dad. Most husbands want to learn how to love their wives more completely and unselfishly. Most dads want (and need) all the tips they can get when it comes to raising children nowadays. They want to be better citizens. And Promise Keepers seems to be getting positive results.

That is not to say, however, that the organization is welcomed in all circles. Far from it. For many people, opposition to Promise Keepers is virulent. They are adamantly opposed to the new men's movement. Interestingly, the opposition is coming from both outside and within Christian circles, and some of it is eye-opening.

CHAPTER 7

PROMISE KEEPERS AND WOMEN

"I almost didn't let my husband come to this conference," Melissa said to me with a mischievous smile. The young woman who I guessed to be in her mid-thirties was a volunteer selling sweatshirts in the Promise Keepers resource tent.

"Why not?" I asked.

"Last night my mom telephoned and said, 'You aren't going to let Pete go, are you?'" Melissa tried to mimic the horror in her mother's voice. "I guess she had read a report in the newspaper that said Promise Keepers are antiwoman, and that they want men to take control of their families. She figured that these guys all think women should be kept in their place, barefoot and pregnant. I tried to tell her that Promise Keepers is supposed to help husbands improve their relationships with their wives.

"My mom said, 'Well, if they really want to improve their relationships with their wives, why don't they allow women to attend? What are they saying inside those stadiums that they don't want women to hear?'"

Melissa's mother's alarm has been echoed by a wide variety of women. Women's groups have presented some of the most serious and highly publicized protests against Promise Keepers. They have picketed outside stadiums at Promise Keepers events; in Chicago a group of women brought along a bass drum to beat as they passed out literature proclaiming that they were not going to be doormats or slaves for men. One protester in the Pontiac Silverdome lobbed a streamer bearing the message REAL MEN DON'T DOMINATE WOMEN. The man who was speaking stopped momentarily and said, "Well, we can all agree on that," and carried on with his message. Women opposed to Promise Keepers have paid pilots to circle stadiums towing derogatory banners from their planes. At one of the first conferences in Boulder, when a plane flew by towing the message: PROMISE BREAKERS NOT PROMISE MAKERS, Bill McCartney stopped short in his talk, and led the men in prayer for the protesters.

At the 1994 Boulder conference a plane circled Folsom Stadium pulling a banner bearing the message: ONLY WEAK MEN ARE AFRAID OF STRONG WOMEN. A few minutes later, the plane returned with a more overt statement: PROMISE KEEPERS, LOSERS AND WEEPERS. Rather than get defensive, the PK group took a different response: As the plane continued circling, the men in the stadium began chanting in response: "Je-sus, JE-SUS, *JE-SUS*! But were the men hearing the criticisms?

Perhaps an even more crucial question is: Do these women's criticisms have merit?

One of the most publicized criticisms of Promise Keepers has to do with its all-male attendance policy. Strictly speaking, Promise Keepers does not exclude women from attending its public conferences. But while women are welcome to volunteer their time and energy to help make the conferences run more smoothly, the event is clearly for men.

A few women have graced the stage at Promise Keepers events, but none have been there as keynote speakers. Those who have been onstage include Dr. Gary Rosberg's wife, Barbara. At the conclusion of Rosberg's talk, in which the licensed marriage counselor publicly confessed that he had not always been the husband and father he should have been, sixty thousand men in the RCA Dome looked on with lumps in their throats as Rosberg washed his wife's feet in an act of contrition and humility. I couldn't help wondering how many of the men would tell their wives about that part of the conference.

Other women have spoken briefly from PK podiums. One such speaker was a woman whose husband had been diagnosed in 1991 with chronic lymphoma. The man, Greg (not his real name), attended the Boulder PK conference in 1993, and there, for the first time, committed his life to Christ. In doing so, he discovered not only the way to live, but the way to die.

Despite his failing health, Greg worked indefatigably throughout 1994, recruiting men to go to Promise Keepers conferences. This enthusiastic Promise Keeper wanted other guys to experience something of the overflowing peace and joy he had discovered. By the time Greg succumbed to the cancer, just prior to the 1994 Anaheim conference, he had influenced more than 350 men to attend Promise Keepers. Consequently, when his wife walked onto the stage at Anaheim, a mere fourteen days after Greg's death, the fifty thousand men in that stadium spontaneously stood to their feet and honored her with applause.[1]

Normally, however, both speakers and audiences at Promise Keepers events are comprised of men only. In Promise Keepers' promotional materials, as well as in the stadium syllabus, the men-only issue is addressed:

Something special happens when men come together in the name of Jesus Christ. The conferences are designed to address specific men's issues. We have discovered that men are more apt to hear and receive the full instruction of the sessions when they are within an all-male setting.[2]

The official statement also carries the reminder, "One of the primary goals of each conference is to deepen the commitment of men to respect and honor women." The ironic implication is that men can be more open, honest, and vulnerable in front of thousands of strangers than they can be before the women with whom they are supposedly most intimate. That dichotomy intrigues some women and irritates others.

Melanie, married to James for eight years, is fascinated with the synergy between what James learns through Promise Keepers and what is happening in their marriage. "James goes to his weekly PK men's group where the guys open up to and encourage each other to be better husbands, fathers, and more godly men. Then he comes home and puts into practice in our marriage and family relationships those things he's learning through Promise Keepers. I don't think that would happen so readily if he and I were simply attending a social group or some other sort of church group."

James concurs. "Suppose Melanie and I were sitting around a table with friends at a dinner party or even at a Bible study; if I were having a problem with pornography, do you think I could openly say, 'Hey, folks; guess what! I like to look at dirty pictures,' or do you really think we could talk about it? No way! I'd bury that problem beneath a mountain of rationalization, or a pile of sugar and sweetness, charm, sophistication, intellectual conversation, or anything else I could use to cover my true self. But within our PK group, we men can talk about the tough issues, and encourage each other to make the kinds of changes that will be good for our wives and families, as well as for us as individuals. I am all in favor of Promise Keepers' all-guy approach."

On the other hand, Sheila, married to Roger for nine years, admitted, "It bugs me that Roger is telling other guys things at Promise Keepers that he is unable or unwilling to talk to me about. Sometimes I wonder, *Should I be blushing around some of Roger's PK buddies? Do they know more about the intimate details of my life than even my parents or my sisters do?* Roger says that he never gets that specific, but from what I've heard from other wives, it sounds to me like some of the guys get rather loose-lipped!"

When I asked one Promise Keepers volunteer worker about the men-only policy, he casually dismissed the men-women equality issue with a wave of his hand as he responded, "What's the big deal? Women's groups have had exclusive meetings for years."

The big deal, of course, is that most women's groups are relatively small in number. Even a large convocation of women rarely requires more than a 3,000-seat auditorium. No women's group, not even conventions of women's groups, is packing out 70,000-seat stadiums.

Although women are not invited to attend the conference sessions, Promise Keepers do make an impression on many of the women who are working at the stadiums in which PK events are held. Margaret, an attractive security guard employed by the RCA Dome in Indianapolis, has worked long hours of overtime at three Promise Keepers conferences held at that site. "I have never once had one of the Promise Keeper men say anything suggestive to me or try to hit on me in any way. They have been perfect gentlemen."

"How does that compare with the football games and the concert crowds?" I asked her.

Margaret rolled her eyes and replied, "You don't want to know."

Despite the Promise Keepers' good intentions and good impressions, many people remain concerned that the all-male exclusivity actually works against PK's stated goals of helping men be better husbands and fathers. The debate rages even in small towns and cities across America. For instance, when the local newspaper asked her opinion of Promise Keepers, Reverend Sally Jo Snyder, a pastor in New Castle, Pennsylvania, responded that she saw "red flags all over the place" concerning PK. She warned that some of Promise Keepers' language—especially in the writings of Dr. Tony Evans—might suggest violence to men hoping to run their homes the PK way. The paper went on to say:

> Snyder's concern is more over the walls that get built when men and women meet separately to hash things out. She says that the separate, "two-camp thing" (men apart from women) never works.
>
> It is pointless, Snyder said, to discuss the shared life experiences of family, business, church, and government if only a part of the participants are doing the talking.
>
> Speaking as a young woman and a female member of the clergy, Snyder says she believes the tone of Promise Keepers is extremely exclusive.[3]

In a letter to the editor the following week, Cami Schaubroeck, a local woman, responded,

> I was deeply disturbed by the comments of the Rev. Sally Jo Snyder . . . She portrays the Promise Keepers movement as one where men learn to be domineering and violent. This is ludicrous and has no factual base. I

am a wife, a sister, and a daughter of Promise Keeper participants and know many wives whose husbands have attended these rallies. Don't you think we should know firsthand the results of this powerful movement?

Here are the results: My husband has learned how to honor and value and respect me, to be faithful to our marriage, to be a loving role model for our daughters and to follow God's instruction to be the spiritual leader of our home . . . We have seen nothing but positive results.[4]

Even some supporters of Promise Keepers, however, wonder whether filling stadiums for men-only conferences will have long-term benefits to marriage partners. Author Michael McManus, whose books and marriage-building classes are used by thousands of churches, feels that for significant, lasting strengthening of marriages, the wives must be involved in the process at some point, as well.[5]

It is not the men-only policy of Promise Keepers that concerns some women; there are opponents who contend that Promise Keepers is *anti*women, and offer as proof Promise Keepers' strong advocacy of an authoritarian patriarchy within the home. Adding to this is a recurring rumor that Promise Keepers is teaching men to dominate and manipulate women. Rosemary Dempsey, vice president of the National Organization for Women, has been quoted as saying, "The problem is the message . . . that men must take back control of the family, be the head, the boss. It's a not-very-well-cloaked misogynistic message."[6]

Such criticisms stem from passages like those written by the popular PK speaker Tony Evans, pastor of the Oak Cliff

Bible Fellowship in Dallas and chaplain of the Dallas Maver-
icks basketball team. Writing in one of Promise Keepers' most
revered publications, *Seven Promises of a Promise Keeper*,
Evans instructed husbands:

> I can hear you saying, "I want to be a spiritually pure
> man. Where do I start?"
>
> The first thing you do is sit down with your wife and
> say something like this: "Honey, I've made a terrible
> mistake. I've given you my role. I gave up leading this
> family, and I forced you to take my place. Now I must
> reclaim that role."
>
> Don't misunderstand what I'm saying here. I'm not
> suggesting that you *ask* for your role back, I'm urging
> you to *take it back*.[7]

It is the last line, urging men to take back their position of
leadership in the home, that has generated so much heat
toward Evans and PK. Evans continues:

> Unfortunately, however, there can be no compromise
> here. If you're going to lead, you must lead. Be sensi-
> tive. Listen. Treat the lady gently and lovingly. But *lead*!
>
> Having said that, let me direct some carefully cho-
> sen words to you ladies who may be reading this: *Give
> it back!* For the sake of your family and the survival of
> our culture, let your man be a man if he's willing. Pro-
> tect yourself, if you must, by handing the reins back
> slowly; take it one step at a time. But if your husband
> tells you he wants to reclaim his role, let him! God
> never meant for you to bear the load you're carrying.[8]

The load Evans is referring to is what he describes as a
national crisis brought on by "the feminization of the American male." Evans explains:

When I say feminization, I am not talking about sexual preference. I'm trying to describe a misunderstanding of manhood that has produced a nation of "sissified" men who abdicate their role as spiritually pure leaders, thus forcing women to fill the vacuum . . . In many cases, women are forced to shoulder the leadership load alone and carry responsibilities that God never intended them to bear. (After all, if the men won't do it, *someone* must.) In the process, their emotional and physical circuits are being overloaded.[9]

Writing in *The Humanist*, John M. Swomley, professor emeritus at St. Paul School of Theology in Kansas City, and national board member of the American Civil Liberties Union, chairing its church-state committee, calls Tony Evans's position "a vivid illustration of the Promise Keepers' anti-women ideology."[10] Swomley claims that Evans is telling "men how to deal with women," implying that Evans and other Promise Keepers are teaching men to deal harshly or hatefully with their mates.

However, in the pages prior to challenging men to take back their position of leadership within the family, Evans writes about a television special on the subject of juvenile delinquency, in which:

> . . . accusing fingers were pointed at the criminal justice system, an unfair economy, and persistent racism. While each of those issues is worthy of our attention, they are all symptoms of a more serious disease. Let's face it! Economics is no excuse for promiscuity and irresponsibility. And racism doesn't get teenage girls pregnant.
>
> The fact is, if Dad doesn't provide spiritually responsible leadership in the home, baby is in big trouble.

That's what the folks downtown don't understand. Without strong families built on a framework of biblical morality, there is no sum of money—no federal, state, county, or municipal program—that can get us out of the ditch we've fallen into.[11]

Evans then goes on to say that the answer lies in men becoming spiritually pure leaders, pure in their passions and pure in their priorities. Evans says this sort of male purity is exemplified in a man who provides a godly example to his children; it means a dad who is committed to raising his children and willing to give his kids his time. It means, according to Evans, that a spiritually pure man must earn the respect of his mate (and others), and become a man of mercy, stability, and wisdom. Only after laying that groundwork, and on that basis, does Evans encourage men to reclaim their manhood and their leadership position in the home.

Some critics of Promise Keepers seem to understand this message better than others. Jeff Wagenheim, a contributing editor for the *New Age Journal*, covered the PK conference in Texas Stadium. He listened to speakers such as Ed Cole discussing how respect for women is lost when a man pursues sex without love; Wagenheim heard Gary Smalley speaking about men expressing honor to their wives. Wagenheim was puzzled, and wrote:

I'm stunned by all the heartfelt discussions of romance and communication. This doesn't look like a bunch of guys working toward becoming tyrants in their households. Throughout the weekend, as conference speakers delve deeper and deeper into issues that tear couples and families apart—a husband or father being emotionally distant or neglecting his responsibilities are among the common ones—I notice that some of the men seem to be fighting back tears, while a few have no fight left: They're crying freely as the men around them offer the comfort of a touch, an embrace, or a quiet word.[12]

Other critics of Promise Keepers have observed these same elements without regarding them as benign. Donna Minkowitz, who writes frequently on gay issues and the religious right, was sent by *Ms.* magazine to attend a Promise Keepers conference. What's so unusual about that? Nothing, except that Minkowitz bought some men's clothes, applied an artificial mustache and a minimalist goatee, and masqueraded as a teenage boy named "Don Sornaga" to sneak into the men-only event at the St. Petersburg ThunderDome in Florida. In her efforts to conceal her identity, Minkowitz confessed that she squashed her breasts beneath two layers of Ace bandages, a running bra, and an undershirt, and crammed a rolled-up sock in her underpants. Concerned about how she might use the restroom without revealing her secret during the two-day conference, Minkowitz was heartened to see that since it was supposedly "all-male" in the main stadium seating areas, PK had commandeered the women's restrooms to help accommodate the huge crowd of men. They simply taped pieces of paper over the WO so the signs on the restroom doors all read MEN.

Minkowitz was even more heartened when she heard some of the major themes of Promise Keepers. In the article resulting from her "spying," Minkowitz conceded:

Over and over, men are urged to show their emotions, to let go of their anger, to reevaluate how they treat the women in their lives. Six of the eight major speakers emphasize that men's fear of being seen as weak or unimportant—in effect, their fear of being equated with

women—can become a terrible obstacle in all their relationships. I'm struck by how close it all sounds to
feminism.[13]

Minkowitz admitted to being deeply moved by the message of PK speaker Greg Laurie, who talked about people who
carry the same problems from one relationship to the next.

Laurie's speech moves me so strongly. Maybe it's
because he emphatically invokes the notions of conscience, forgiveness, and the capacity to change—
qualities that are hardly ever referred to by Jerry
Falwell or Pat Robertson or, for that matter, by the left-
ists and gay liberationists who've been my closest com-
rades.[14]

But then the tone turns more cynical. What bothered
Minkowitz was Promise Keepers' conviction that there is a
divinely inspired "order" in which families are designed to
function best. Promise Keepers teaches the biblical principles
that parents should have authority over their dependent children, and that while husbands and wives should submit to
one another, a husband is the head of the wife—as Christ is
the head of the church, and gave himself up for the church
(see Ephesians 5:21–25).

The problem, as Minkowitz sees it, is that,

The Promise Keepers spend the bulk of their time
teaching men how to refrain from abusing because they
believe men ought to be good masters, not abusive
ones. They don't doubt for a moment that the ultimate
responsibility for the world—for men's and women's
lives both—is men's. This fantasy of benevolent domination is at the core of the Promise Keepers' vision . . .
To the Promise Keepers, patriarchal power is legitimate

and, in fact, desirable, so long as it is not "misused." In their fantasy, everyone can remain in their place—men at the "head" of the family, and women behind—so long as men are kind and good. Women are innocent but inferior creatures who depend on men's benevolent stewardship.[15]

Promise Keepers maintains a stoic silence in the face of such criticism. Not that its representatives don't answer the questions. They do, Indeed, they are probably exhausted trying to explain Tony Evans's comments for the umpteenth time. But it seems that PK's answer to charges that it is promoting sexism provide little real information, beyond reiterating the scriptural doctrine of "headship," which states that the man should be the head of the family—by becoming the servant to the family.

At a 1996 Promise Keepers press conference in Indianapolis, I waited and waited for the subject to surface. It never did, so I brought it up. I mentioned feminist charges that Promise Keepers are encouraging misogynistic attitudes among its men, and asked what PKs' position was concerning this matter. Instead of receiving a straightforward answer to my question, I was told to read a book, *Strategies for a Successful Marriage* by Promise Keepers' vice president of ministry advancement, E. Glenn Wagner, and to watch and listen to the Saturday morning presentation by Gary Rosberg, both of which I was happy to do. But that still did not answer my questions, or the feminist accusations.

On the other hand, most of the women with whom I talked concerning Promise Keepers agree that PK makes no mention of male domination and manipulation of women, and in fact espouses the opposite by encouraging men to take responsibility for the spiritual life of their family members.

"Sexism is a nonissue here," said Sheryl, a photographer for a newspaper covering PK. "I have photographed several of these events, and anyone who says these guys are sexist just hasn't been there, or else is hearing what they want to hear through their own headphones."

Even some outspoken critics of Promise Keepers see immense value in PK's emphasis upon men caring for the family, emotional expression, and personal ethics. For instance, Jeff Wagenheim quotes Priscilla Inkpen, a United Church of Christ minister in Boulder, as saying, "It's difficult to be 100 percent critical of the Promise Keepers. I think they are speaking to an important need: for men to take responsibility. A lot of men need to learn that, and Promise Keepers seems to be touching a nerve with many. But . . . you have to ask: What nerve are they touching? Is it men's hunger to be present in their relationships with their wives and children? Or is it the hunger to be on top?"[16]

Most women PK-watchers who do not consider themselves radical feminists dismiss criticism that suggests Promise Keepers is teaching men to lead women back into some sort of subservient status. "That has to be a smoke screen for some other agenda," counters Sylvia, a thirty-eight-year-old who formerly supported radical feminist causes. Today Sylvia is a high-school English teacher who has volunteered at two PK conferences. When I asked her about the feminist criticisms of Promise Keepers, Sylvia replied, "Frankly, I think such criticisms reflect a basic fear and insecurity on the part of some women. They think, 'All those guys getting together—and without us! What are they up to? What are they talking about? It must be something sinister.' How foolish."

Marlene, a mother of two grown young women, has volunteered at four Promise Keepers events in three separate locations around the country. She confessed that she had strong misgivings before her first up-close contact with Promise Keepers. "I was concerned for my daughters, mostly. Their husbands were involved with the movement, so I decided to check it out for myself. What I discovered was that our sons-in-law, men who were reluctant to form fast friendships, suddenly let down their defenses and not only opened up to other Promise Keepers, but more importantly, became much more open and better communicators with my daughters. I've been sold on PK ever since."

During the early stages of my research for this book, I went to a restaurant to eat dinner following a Promise Keepers weekend. While waiting to be seated at a table, I was quickly pegged as "one of them" by a woman standing in line behind me. I wondered how she could tell that I had been to the stadium, and I was about to ask her—there was no telltale smell of spilled beer on my tennis shoes, as has often been true following many NFL games I have attended—when I noticed that my Promise Keepers media pass was still clipped to my shirt pocket.

The woman was carrying a briefcase and wearing an expensive-looking business suit. I soon found out that the woman's husband had also attended the conference. "Aren't you a little afraid that he is going to come home and try to make you wash the dishes, run the vacuum cleaner, and clean the commode?" I asked her only partly in jest.

"Are you kidding?" she replied. "He went to Promise Keepers last year and when he came home, I almost had to fight with him to let me do any of the housework. On top of that, he wanted to talk . . . and talk . . . and talk. You have to understand, before going to Promise Keepers, it strained my husband to talk to me or the kids for ten minutes after dinner at night. Now, I can hardly keep up with him! And he doesn't just want to discuss his day; he wants to know what I'm feeling, what my hopes and dreams are. Every once in a while, I feel like checking his driver's license to make sure this is the same guy who used to live at our house."

That woman's response may be the most typical of all. Indeed, most wives of Promise Keepers are quick to sing the organization's praises. "We get back stronger men than we send!" is a common assertion of many spouses of Promise Keepers.

For instance, when Mary Ann drove her recently retired husband, Gene, to the church parking lot to board a bus to the Charlotte conference, Gene complained all the way. "I don't want to go to this thing. I have so much work to do at home; I can't afford to blow the whole weekend listening to God-talk."

"He was so down," Mary Ann recalls, "that I almost said, 'Well, let's turn around and go home.' But I didn't. I felt strongly that Gene should go to the conference. He seemed so indifferent not just to Promise Keepers, but to all of life. His eyes were hollow and his face looked tired and sallow.

"When he came back, I was sure somebody had pumped him full of vitamin B-12! He looked and acted ten years younger. He had a smile on his face, a twinkle in his eyes, and a lilt in his step that I had not seen for years. He looked as though he was walking on air. I don't know what they did to Gene at that conference, but if they could bottle it, they'd be billionaires."

Although PK's emphasis is on married men, single men and teenage boys are welcome at PK events. So are divorced men. In fact, 21 percent of the men who attend the conferences have been divorced at least once. Most hope to remarry. By incorporating the lessons they have learned at PK, they also hope to greatly reduce the risk of future marital woes.

"I messed up my first marriage rather badly," lamented

Bob, a Nashville recording studio engineer. "I worked long hours—often into the wee hours of the morning—trying to help someone else produce a hit record. By the time I got home, my family was either in bed, or I was too exhausted to enjoy being with them. Finally, my wife took our three children and left. She said she didn't want to be married to someone who was already married—to a recording studio.

"When the guys at my church invited me to go to the Memphis Promise Keepers conference, I was interested, but I figured the last thing I wanted to hear was a day and a half of speakers talking about husband-wife relationships. But the guys talked me into going along—as our designated single person—and I was pleasantly surprised at what I heard. The concepts that PK taught that weekend applied to both married and single men. In fact, I wish somebody would have told me some of those things before I ever got married. I may not have hurt the woman I loved."

Rather than wanting to fight with Promise Keepers, many women want to join them. An average of 48 percent of PK's 3,300 volunteers at each stadium conference are women. According to the organization's magazine, *The PK Volunteer*, "At any given conference, 1,200–1,300 women volunteers work four-hour shifts to fill close to 7,000 positions."[17]

Undoubtedly, some women volunteer simply to get an inside look at a men-only PK conference. Others want to experience what the men are experiencing. The overwhelming majority, however, volunteer because they are convinced Promise Keepers is doing something important in the lives of men.

Even more impressive are the droves of women who spend hours in concerted prayer for the Promise Keepers conferences. At every stadium event, somewhere hidden in the catacombs beneath or behind the playing field, a group of women gather in a "prayer room" to pray for the Promise Keepers event taking place in the main arena. Long before the men arrive at the stadium, the women are already there praying for them. During every hour of the conference, and often long into the night, the women work in shifts, taking turns praying for the men in the seats, the speakers, the wives back home, and any special needs or crises that occur during the conference. Men are welcome to pray too, but the majority of the "prayer warriors" are women. Most PK leaders attribute much of their success in the public rallies to the prayers of these women.

A frequent visitor in the prayer room is none other than Coach McCartney himself, as he personally requests prayer for various aspects of the conferences. In one 1996 conference, McCartney showed up in the prayer room around midday on Saturday with a troubled look on his face. He was concerned that the conference was not going well, that the number of men who had responded to the Friday night invitation was unusually low compared to the number who had "gone forward" in the previous year. He was also perplexed that a scant thirty-one boys out of nearly three thousand had accepted Christ after a powerful message during the youth breakout session.

McCartney asked the women to pray. "The conference results are in your hands," McCartney told the women. "What happens in this room is crucial to what will happen on the floor."

After Coach McCartney left the room, the women began praying more intensely.

Approximately fifteen minutes later, Kathy Blume, wife of PK senior events manager Bob Blume, came into the prayer room. Kathy was unaware of what had been happening in the room, but she had good news. She reported that a highly

Not just another day at the ballpark. Men are packing Promise Keepers stadium conferences across the United States, and will soon be doing so in twenty other countries. Nearly 1.2 million men went to PK events in 1996.

The mood is often jubilant at Promise Keepers, similar to a sporting event, as men freely express what they like and what they don't.

Thom Hickling

Bill McCartney, former University of Colorado head football coach, is the controversial founder and CEO of Promise Keepers.

Brent Pirie and Norman Seow

Promise Keepers teaches men to express their feelings toward their wives. Apparently these men have caught on.

This man's T-shirt typifies some of the questions being raised about Promise Keepers.

The Pittsburgh all-male PK choir, sporting their REAL MEN SING REAL LOUD T-shirts, helps generate crowd enthusiasm.

PK attracts a wide variety of men to its conferences.

What could be better than mixing God and country—snoozing during another PK speech, or simply catching some rays in the warm afternoon sun?

Two men embrace in tears responding to PK's call to tear down the walls of racism.

Tony Evans, the Dallas area pastor whose advice to men that they take back their leadership role in their families inflamed feminists.

Thom Hickling

Brent Pirie and Norman Seow

Although only a small percentage of Promise Keepers are nonwhites, PK is hoping to increase the number of men of color at its conferences.

A poignant moment as a wheelchair-bound Promise Keeper raises his hand in prayer and praise to God.

Thom Hickling

The little-known key to Promise Keepers' success: Throughout every stadium conference, a group of women is praying on-site.

Most Promise Keepers are eighteen years of age and older, but many fathers want their much younger sons to experience PK.

PK can be a confusing contradiction for some people.

Men praying for other men is an important part of every Promise Keepers event.

This Promise Keeper pauses for a quiet moment of solitude and meditation, even though he is among thousands of other men.

Men respond in a wide variety of ways to PK's message. This man is so overwhelmed that he bows his face to the stadium floor as another man prays for him.

Brent Pirie and Norman Seow

Thom Hickling

A son and his father, carrying a bag of materials purchased at the PK resource tent, move toward the stage for a closer look.

Promise Keepers continues to unite men around a spiritual focus. Will it survive? These men signal a resounding Yes!

Thom Hickling

respected, deeply spiritual older gentleman had said that the entire tenor of the conference had begun to change . . . about fifteen minutes previously.

Dian Ginter, a twenty-eight-year prayer veteran from Highland, California, who frequently manages the prayer room at Promise Keepers events, told me of a rather unusual practice she often incorporates. At many conferences, Ginter enlists a male volunteer to sit in a chair while a group of women (and men, if they are available) gather around him to pray. The man in the middle will then begin to confess the corporate sins of the men who have gathered in the stadium, as well as his own. He confesses hate, lust, greed, adultery (whether he has been guilty of those things or not), and a plethora of other moral and spiritual failures—all on behalf of the men in the stands.

He asks God's forgiveness for not keeping his wife and children as priorities. He admits to not having been there for them; he admits to having allowed his work or something else to interfere with his relationship to God and his family. All the while, the people praying in the circle are asking God that those same powerful holds on the lives of the men in the stadium will be broken. And in many cases, PK evangelism volunteers report, they are.

Dian Ginter takes it all in stride. "We believe that God hears and answers our prayers, and that what happens on the floor of the stadium [i.e., the response of the men] takes place first in the prayer room, as we pray." Indeed, the PK women usually arrive at the stadium well before the men.

Early Friday afternoon at many conferences, before the gates are open to the men, women walk throughout the stadium, praying. In Indianapolis, for example, I saw half a dozen women walking the aisles of the RCA Dome, praying briefly at each section of the 62,000-seat stadium, often pausing to pray over an individual seat for the man who would occupy it that night and the following day.

Another ritual, initiated at the 1996 Clergy Conference in Atlanta and rapidly becoming a behind-the-scenes PK tradition, is the reading of the Bible in the stadium—the whole Bible, word for word, from Genesis to Revelation. How do they do that? Around noon on Friday, while sound engineers are still testing the sound system and other workers are going about their last-minute preparations, a group of volunteers, predominantly women, gather to receive their Scripture assignments. The entire Bible is divided into sections and each person assigned a specific passage to be read in a designated area of the stadium. The volunteers then spread throughout the stadium, into each area where activity will later take place, from the stage to the press box. There, each person reads his or her portion of Scripture and prays for the people who will be active in that part of the stadium. In a half hour to forty-five minutes, depending upon the number of volunteers, the entire Bible—all 1,500-plus pages—is read throughout the stadium.

One woman told me, "With all the prayer going on in the stadium, accompanied by the reading of the Bible, it is as though God's presence just permeates the whole place. No wonder the guys notice something different the moment they walk in here. God has already been here waiting for them."

Since women are so interested in Promise Keepers, why not start a separate branch of the movement especially to address women's issues and needs? "That's not in our present game plan," says a PK executive. When asked by women to begin such a group, Promise Keepers points thumbs down and reiterates its original mission statement: Promise Keepers is dedicated to uniting *men* through vital relationships, and helping them to become godly influences in their world. It's men who have messed things up historically, PK says, and if we can help the guys get it together with God and each other, we will be indirectly helping their wives and children as well.

Not surprisingly, some women have taken what may be the next logical step—a Promise Keepers–type of group for women. One of the earliest groups organized was founded in Denver in 1993, calling themselves (I am not joking here) "Suitable Helpers." In 1996, the group was going strong, growing slowly but surely. About 180 women attended the Suitable Helpers conference in 1996, held in the Indianapolis suburb of Greenwood a week before the Indy Promise Keepers conference. Similar to PK gatherings, the women sang, prayed, and listened to speakers address subjects to help them be—what else?—suitable helpers to their husbands.

Similar organizations have sprung up in other cities. Houston—where six hundred women maintained a week-long prayer vigil prior to and during the 1995 PK conference—is home to the "Promise Reapers." Wichita, Kansas, has the "Heritage Keepers," and women in Pasadena can now be known as "Chosen Women," if they choose.

In addition to new parachurch women's groups, many local churches are reporting a resurgence of interest in women's ministries within the church, a phenomenon pastors often link directly to the impact of Promise Keepers. The leaders of these women's groups are quick to point out that their organizations are not sprouting in opposition to Promise Keepers, nor are they threatened by anything Promise Keepers espouses.

Betsy, a woman who has long been active in women's prayer groups, explains, "For years, women in the church griped because their men were not involved in the spiritual side of the church, family, and community. Now, thanks largely to Promise Keepers, we are finally getting some strong male spiritual leadership, and we simply want to support what the men are doing, and better prepare ourselves to respond to that."

Despite the rancorous protests of a few feminist-leaning groups, Promise Keepers continues to draw rave reviews from most women. Catherine, a distinguished woman in her fifties, is convinced that PK's work has validity. She saw Promise Keepers' impact up-close in the life of her son-in-law.

Catherine told me, "Ron was so career-minded, I was afraid that he was forgetting that he had a wife—my daughter—and a little baby. But I was trying not to interfere, even when I saw him becoming consumed by what seemed to me to be an insatiable desire for more and more material things. Ron prided himself in being able to provide so well for his family, but actually, I think he was more interested in providing for himself. He was good at his work, so he was rapidly rising in the corporate world, but I could see that his long hours and short weekends were taking a toll on my daughter.

"The men at their church invited Ron to go along with them to a Promise Keepers meeting. There he heard a speaker talking about how foolish it would be to gain the fame and fortune of the world but lose his own family and, worse yet, his own soul. When Ron came home, I noticed a profound change in him. Almost overnight, he went from being a selfish, career-obsessed workaholic to a giving, caring man who cannot seem to spend enough time with his family. I don't know what-all Promise Keepers is doing, but I hope they keep on doing it."

More than a few women see Promise Keepers as a tremendous aid in drawing the men in their families back to the church, and eventually back to God. At one PK event, I met Jennifer, a woman in her late fifties who works for Promise Keepers in the organization's Denver headquarters. Jennifer's job requires her to travel a great deal to various PK functions around the country, so her semiretired husband travels with her. He, however, is not a believer.

"I pray for him all the time," Jennifer told me. "He comes to the conferences with me, but he has never sat down among the men. He always sits in the guest sections, which is not quite the same as being right in the middle of all the excitement. It is frustrating to me that he could be so close to all that God is doing through Promise Keepers, yet be unaffected by it himself. However, he has started attending church with me when we are home. And I'm praying that someday soon my husband will be a Promise Keeper in reality, not just because he is married to me."

Promise Keepers' president, Randy Phillips, sums up the mutual appreciation between PK and women. "The strongest proponents of Promise Keepers are the wives, mothers, sisters, and daughters of the men who attend. They know that the man who comes back to them is not trying to misuse or impose his masculine authority. He's a man who wants to give, serve, listen, honor, and care. Women see the positive change and realize the influence it will have in their lives and families. They tell their friends, 'You better send Charlie! Look what's happening to my George.'"[18]

Because Promise Keepers has been eliciting praise from many wives, moms, and sisters, it tends to ignore the protests of a few malcontents. After all, there were more than 72,000 men inside the Pontiac Silverdome, and hardly a dozen protesters outside the stadium. PK's attitude seems to be, "If the media want to make a big deal out of a marginal group, that is their prerogative, but we will focus on more pressing issues."

One of those pressing issues on which the leaders of Promise Keepers have dealt straightforwardly is the charge that PK is a racist, white man's religious club. It is a charge that Bill McCartney takes seriously.

CHAPTER 8

ARE PROMISE KEEPERS RACISTS?

"Promise Keepers? Ha! I've heard Whitey's promises before," said Derik, a Tuscarora Native American from near Niagara Falls. "Why would I want to go to a Promise Keepers conference? That's a white man's god and a white man's party."

Bill McCartney has often heard charges similar to Derik's, and he cringes when anyone accuses Promise Keepers of racism: playing to white, Anglo-Saxon, Protestant crowds, rather than men of all ethnic cultures and economic strata. Racism is a matter close to McCartney's heart, and his passion for racial reconciliation dates back to the early days of Promise Keepers.

McCartney traces his own deeper understanding of racial issues to the mid-1980s funeral of Teddy Woods, a black Denver attorney who had once played football at the University of Colorado. Although McCartney had visited in the homes of many athletes of color, attempting to recruit them for his football teams, the former coach confessed that he understood little about the pain people of color endure in America. But at

Teddy Woods's funeral, McCartney was for the first time stirred by an anguish for people of other races. How McCartney could have lived in America for nearly half a century before he saw the pain of black people—especially having met with many young men of color and their families in their own homes—mystifies even Coach Mac himself. He offers no excuse but ignorance.

McCartney's stand for reconciliation actually predates his involvement with Promise Keepers. He was, for example, the only head coach of a National Collegiate Athletic Association Division 1-A football team to have as many men of color on his coaching staff as he had whites.

In 1991, McCartney stood onstage at one of PK's first large assemblies, in which more than 4,200 men had gathered at the basketball arena on the campus of the University of Colorado. The day was a sensational fulfillment of the original seventy Promise Keepers' dream to have such a convocation of men, and already the PK leaders had begun looking forward to filling Folsom Stadium with fifty thousand men the following year. Looking back, McCartney admits to having been exuberant. "We were slapping high fives in the background, saying, 'God is moving here!' "

When it came time for McCartney to speak, he had a revelation. McCartney says, "I felt like the Lord spoke to me and he said, 'Look at the audience here, and what do you see?'

"I said, 'Lord, I see the Spirit of the Living God coming alive in these men. Lord, I thank you for what you've done here today.'

" 'What else do you see?' "

McCartney spoke sheepishly. "Well, Lord, they're almost all white guys . . ."

All day long, McCartney and his colleagues had been telling the men in the arena that if each of them recruited just one man every month, they could fill the Folsom football stadium the following year.

Then came the epiphany that changed McCartney's focus and that of Promise Keepers. McCartney claims that God said to him, "You tell them you can put fifty thousand guys in that stadium, but if we don't have a full and fair representation of my people, if the men of color are not here, you guys can all be there, but I'm not coming."

Bill McCartney delivered the message he felt that he had heard from God, but to his deep chagrin it met with the enthusiasm you'd expect for a dislodged porta-potty. In the weeks following the conference, McCartney began getting mail from some of the men who were in the arena that day. The letters were not kind, gracious words of encouragement, congratulating him for his courage in speaking to the racial issue. On the contrary, the letters scolded and challenged McCartney: "What you said is not scripturally sound. The Bible itself says 'Where two or more are gathered in my [Jesus'] name, I am there.' What right do you have to get up and say this?"[1]

Being accustomed to Monday morning quarterbacks, Coach McCartney was not greatly shaken by the negative letters. More importantly, he felt that he had obeyed God by addressing the volatile issue of racial unity. McCartney stood by his message. Still, he was surprised at the reluctance on the part of so many Christian men to deal with what to him was a clear mandate from God. What possible excuse could Christians have for being unwilling to mingle with other races when they serve the same Jesus, friend to all? Was Christ not enough to bind them together?

McCartney was about to find out.

Over a period of about three months, McCartney's travels were to take him to five major cities to spread the word about Promise Keepers' original vision of reaching men. Still coaching at Colorado, McCartney made no claims to be a preacher, so in preparation for his speaking tour, he spent a great deal of time working on his speeches, praying and asking God what message he should present: "As I would go into my prayer room and get down on my knees and beg Almighty God to give me a message that I could share in major cities around the country, the message that God put on my heart was a message of what God felt in his heart about racism."[2]

Racism? Few white Christian leaders were talking about racism in 1993. Converting the masses, political involvement, new translations of the Bible, Christians in the media, building bigger churches, new television programs . . . all sorts of exciting things were being discussed by Christian leaders privately and publicly. But you could count on one hand the prominent white preachers who regularly hit upon racism as an issue, much less as a sin. Not even the venerable Billy Graham directly addressed racism from his Crusade pulpits, except perhaps as an aside.

Now McCartney, having just given birth to the most rapidly growing men's movement in the world, was going to risk blowing it by talking on a sensitive subject that obviously nobody wanted to hear about. No wonder that McCartney said later, "I wept many times as I forged out this message."[3]

He went first to Indianapolis to speak to a group of 1,200 men in a church. The coach's initial reception was overwhelming; the excitement and anticipation to hear how Coach McCartney and others were planning to bring men together for a giant conference in a football stadium was electric. When McCartney got up to speak, the men gave him a standing ovation for over five minutes before he even said a word. "Then I spoke the message that God had put on my heart, and—so help me this is true—when I got done speaking, not a single guy applauded. There was tremendous disappointment in the majority of the guys out there. They were stung by my remarks."[4]

Confused by this response, and certain that he must have misunderstood what God wanted him to do, McCartney went back to Boulder to reevaluate his message. Says McCartney, "I lifted my hands toward the Lord and said, 'Lord, I missed your heart! How did I do that?'"

Once again, McCartney's mail bristled with disappointed, angry letters from men who disagreed with his message or his approach, or both. "Guys said, 'I drove two hundred miles to go to that gathering. If you were going to talk about that crap, you should have advertised it.'

"But I didn't hear anything more from the Lord except, 'Be obedient.' "[5]

McCartney went on to Anaheim and received a similarly dismal response. Next came Denver, just down the road from Boulder, a place where people of color are rare, except on the university campus, and where McCartney's reputation for being outspoken was expected. But when the coach began talking about trying to reconcile the races, the reaction was once again the same. Blank expressions stared back at him as men sat scratching their heads and saying, "What was that all about?"

Portland, Oregon, was McCartney's last stop on his five-city swing. A group of community leaders met him at his plane and said, "Coach, we just had a Billy Graham Crusade here and . . . we don't have a problem here with racism; everybody's together."[6]

Once again McCartney was greeted as a conquering hero . . . until he began to speak. The men in Portland responded basically the same way the men in Indianapolis had—as long as McCartney talked about men being strong leaders in the family, better husbands and fathers, and better Christian representatives to the world, he was met with rousing enthusiasm. The moment he began discussing racial reconciliation, it was as though someone pulled the shades down and put blinders on the men in the audience.

When McCartney finished speaking in Portland, he sat down while the men eyed him icily. Finally, a distinguished-looking, sixty-year-old black man walked out of the audience to the podium. Tears streamed down his face as he spoke into the microphone. "I never thought in my lifetime that I would hear a white man say what's been said here today. Maybe there is hope."

The last four words resonated within McCartney's heart.

McCartney recalls, "When he said those four words, the Holy Spirit of God came on me like you can't believe, and validated me, and said, 'Yes! You have been speaking my heart! Keep speaking what I have put on your heart!' "[7]

McCartney and his men have continued to make racial reconciliation a major tenet of Promise Keepers' overall message, emphasizing service-oriented, practical involvement in communities. Skeptics both inside the PK movement and without have wondered aloud how much of McCartney's passion to see racial healing stems from having to come to grips with his daughter's interracial relationships with Sal Aunese and Shannon Clavelle. McCartney is, after all, the grandfather of two "boys of color."

Regardless of what initially spawned the reconciliation thrust—the assuaging of personal guilt, divine direction, or a desire to grapple with an already difficult family situation— Bill McCartney has consistently and passionately led the charge in tearing down walls of racial bitterness and resentment. Ironically, when he resigned as coach after the 1994 season and "his longtime assistant Bob Simmons was passed over for a less-experienced white replacement, McCartney sided with an unlikely ally, the Reverend Jesse Jackson, in charging racism."[8] In 1996 alone, Coach Mac visited more than forty cities, meeting with small groups of black men, seeking not only their support of Promise Keepers, but a better understanding of how PK might help build bridges between the races. For the most part, McCartney's reception among these groups was cool at best.

Nevertheless, Promise Keepers' emphasis upon racial reconciliation sets it apart from most other high-profile Christian ministries. Unquestionably, it also earns the movement much positive press, especially among reporters who otherwise might shun PK's religious message. But because racism is an issue that even nonreligious people recognize to be rearing its venomous head with increasing frequency and violence, there is an openness to hear out what Promise Keepers has to say. The attitude among many is, "At least Promise Keepers is trying to do something."

Promise Keepers couches its racial-harmony message in soft terms, using phrases such as "racial reconciliation" rather than "racial equality." It avoids talking about most of the tough issues, such as jobs for men of color, drugs in the community, and access to better education and housing opportunities, choosing instead to focus on the spiritual aspects of these problems. Promise Keepers continually reiterates, concerning racial as well as other issues, that "only by changing people's hearts" can society truly be changed. Few people ever argue with the truth of that statement, but Promise Keepers' propensity to provide spiritual answers to practical problems sometimes comes across as stonewalling. But then, PK makes no claims of being primarily a social action group; it is essentially a spiritual movement, and therefore addresses issues of racial and denominational reconciliation as part of its *spiritual* responsibility.

Indeed, when the Promise Keepers board of directors met to decide the theme of their 1996 conferences, after bandying about many possibilities, they finally settled on "Break Down the Walls." Explaining their rationale, E. Glenn Wagner, PK's vice president of ministry advancement, said, "The issue was to address proactively what it means to go past the barriers that separate us, not only denominationally but racially. To call oneself a Christian, and to promote racism, either by our ignorance or by our blatant activity, is a sin against God."[9]

At each conference in 1996, speakers addressed the subjects of husband-wife relationships, parent-child relationships, support for pastors, and the typical assortment of topics tied to the Seven Promises. But the main emphasis was upon racial reconciliation. Trumpeting the theme as loudly as anyone was Bill McCartney.

In all of his talks around America in 1996, McCartney managed to squeeze in a message similar to that which he gave the men in Pittsburgh:

Look around this stadium tonight. Where are the men of color? Why are there not more men of color here? I think I can tell you the answer. There is a spirit of white racial superiority that exists in our land. Hear me now! Hear what I want to share with you. I have traveled our nation. For the last year I have been in forty-three cities, meeting with men of color. I have listened to their hearts, and I have heard their pain . . . I want to share with you that white racial superiority can be defined as insensitivity to the pain of the people of color. We do not look at their pain; we have not washed their feet like Jesus said, privately and publicly. We have not been willing to do that . . . How would you like it if you had to come to the company of someone every day who thought they were better than you? How many of you know what that is like, to work in that kind of environment? Can I share with you that we as white guys, if we found ourselves in that kind of predicament, we would get another job? We would go somewhere else. The men and women of color are strapped. They can't go anywhere else.[10]

Again and again, in one city after another, McCartney hammered home his point. As he did in most cities where PK held a stadium event, McCartney told the press before the Denver conference in Mile High Stadium, "The sin of racism is insidious and ingrained in the fabric of our society. It comes from a notion of white racial superiority—and the sin lies in that we do nothing about it. America won't be able to break down the walls until we confront racism head on."[11]

At that same press conference, Reverend A. R. Bernard, an African American pastor of a five-thousand-member Brooklyn inner-city church, and a featured Promise Keepers speaker, recognized that racism went both ways, from whites toward blacks, and from blacks toward whites. Said Bernard, "White America needs to repent [of] attitudes of racial superiority, and blacks need to repent [of] years of bitterness, hatred, and anger."[12]

Pittsburgh pastor Joseph Garlington, also an African American, echoed those sentiments at a press conference prior to the Pittsburgh PK event. Garlington said, "Often, there is a political concept that racism is something that only white folks are capable of. But it's a two-way street, and everybody must take responsibility for hatred." Later that day, speaking to a potentially drowsy after-lunch crowd, in the middle of a sweltering July afternoon, Garlington nonetheless held the PK men spellbound as he addressed his topic of building bridges between the races. He introduced one of his closest friends and accountability partners, Gary Mitrik, a white pastor from the suburban Pittsburgh area. The two men stood arm-in-arm on the PK stage while the men in the stands cheered heartily.

The largely white crowd came unglued when Garlington explained why he did not attend the "Million Man March" in Washington, D.C., a gathering of men of color led by Nation of Islam leader Louis Farrakhan in October of that year.

"I wouldn't go because you weren't invited," Garlington said, as he pointed to white men in the crowd. "It would have been an act of disloyalty to go stand in a place where you couldn't go and I couldn't say you are my brother."

The predominantly white crowd collectively leaped to its feet, giving Garlington a prolonged standing ovation. Several black members of the audience later panned Garlington's remarks as being self-serving. "Would he have said something like that if there were forty thousand black guys and only five thousand white guys sitting in the stands?" one of the men asked. "I doubt it. If you ask me, Garlington was simply pandering to the white guys. How does that help to reconcile the races?"[13]

Garlington, however, had hit upon a key element of Promise Keepers' racial reconciliation emphasis, one which is often neglected by other groups with similar goals: namely, that racism goes both ways. Nonwhites can have bitter racist attitudes toward Caucasians just as much as whites can have toward men of color. All three of Promise Keepers' premier spokesmen for racial reconciliation—Garlington, Tony Evans, and Wellington Boone—deal straightforwardly with the need for dual responsibility when discussing the issue of racism.

If Garlington is the more eloquent, thought-provoking PK promoter of racial reconciliation, Tony Evans is the master at combining a bombastic, "traditional" black preacher style, with a finely chiseled message that appeals to men across the spectrum. Stressing the need for reconciliation now, Evans told a group of Promise Keepers, "There is no time left for racism; there is no time left for culturalism; there is no time left for elitism. When you are in a war, you don't care about the color, class, or culture of the man fighting next to you as long as he is shootin' in the same direction you are. And we're in a war!" Driving home his message in his throaty, evocative style, Evans rocked the stadium as he shouted, "We may have all come to this country on different ships, but we [are] all in the same boat now! And that is trying to save our wives, and our children, and our families."[14]

A third black Promise Keepers' spokesman for racial reconciliation is Wellington Boone, who combines Garlington's intellectual prowess and articulate approach with Evans's ability to hype the crowd through vocal gymnastics and street talk. Boone grew up in the ghetto, but when Wellington was still a boy, a white man helped him place his trust in Jesus. Boone escaped the poverty and obscurity of the "hood," but he has not forgotten it.

Onstage and off, Boone, too, stresses the need for mutual repentance and reconciliation between the races. "To the black brothers, I say . . . you can't wait till people seek your forgiveness, you have to initiate forgiveness. Because as long as you carry hatred, God cannot promote that spirit. Jesus forgave us by dying for us, before we ever asked him for it."[15]

Boone possesses a fiery charisma. He wears his sincerity on his sleeve, and if anyone happens to miss it, he will be glad to take off his jacket and show you. He comes across as streetwise yet guileless. If he has a fault, it is his propensity to start preaching every time he sees a microphone. During a press conference in Indianapolis, I watched the media's eyes glaze over as Boone began explaining in profound and some-what confusing spiritual terms why racism was such a prob-lem in America. Boone said:

> When we look at the history of the church, we have to ask ourselves why two thousand years after the resur-rection of Jesus Christ we are still guilty [in the areas of] racial reconciliation and denominational unity, when Jesus prayed his high priestly prayer in John 17, and the outpouring of the Holy Spirit at Pentecost, there emphasized the fulfillment of the redemptive work of Jesus, in the sense that he made them all one. That was one of the things that came about as a result of it. Now, here we are, two thousand years later . . . instead of generational progression, to me it has been generational regression. The essence of Jesus' prayer was that we would be one even as he was one with the Father. So the issue of racism is not an issue of unity between cultures; it is an issue of carnality in the church. First Corinthians 3 says, "If there are divi-sions and envy and jealousies among you, are you not carnal and walk as men?" So while we emphasize the need for cultural unity, there is a real need for spiritual growth . . .[16]

"Say what?" the guy sitting next to me asked, dumb-founded. On my other side was a female radio reporter des-perately trying to take notes on Boone, recording his statement, hoping for anything that might make for a sound bite. After a while, she simply shut off her recorder, closed her notepad, and sat listening, confused but mesmerized. "I don't understand a thing he is saying," she whispered to me, "but he says it so passionately, I feel I must listen."

Despite his tendency to communicate in Christianspeak,

Wellington Boone remains a formidable force among the PK advocates of racial reconciliation. The man is not afraid to speak his mind. In an interview with *Ministries Today,* a magazine geared toward Christian pastors and ministry leaders, Boone pulled out the stops, lamenting, "The pillars that uphold black America are crumbling. Everywhere there is disintegration, drug addiction, destruction of the family, resurgence of racial tension. The black community has raised leaders to the national level, but they are not bringing the message of life. Often, unfortunately, neither is the church . . . I often ask young people, 'Are you waiting for another Martin Luther King, or are you going to become one yourselves?' "[17]

One of the few modern black leaders who sees the book *Uncle Tom's Cabin* in a positive light ("Uncle Tom had a real revelation of heaven. He was able to forgive his tormenters . . . What a role model for unqualified love!"), Boone does not view racial reconciliation as something a white culture bestows upon people of color. He says, "Our challenge isn't in being accepted by whites. We're already accepted by God. We need to break out of this ethnic mindset. It's all right to be ethnically *conscious*, but not to be ethnically *controlled*. My world view must come from the kingdom [of God], not from my culture."[18]

When I asked Wellington Boone what he would say to the men of color who attended Louis Farrakhan's Million Man March, Boone replied, "I'd say that we love them. Jesus loves them." Boone went on, "Eighty percent of the men who attended Farrakhan's Million Man March were Christians . . . In terms of Promise Keepers: our emphasis is Jesus."

Alluding to Promise Keepers' cancelled million-man demonstration in Washington, planned for 1996 but then rescheduled it to avoid looking as though PK had a political agenda in a presidential election year, Boone said, "I believe Farra-

khan got his idea for a million-man march from Coach Mc-
Cartney, who has been talking about it for five years."[19]

Boone continued, "Some black people say that [PK] is a
white . . . counterpart to Farrakhan's black movement and
that is not true. We are emphasizing all races; we are emphasizing all denominations."[20]

At that point, PK's national spokesperson, Steve Chavis, an
African American himself, jumped in and said, "There is no
competition between Promise Keepers and the Million Man
March. They are completely different."[21]

Boone concluded, "This is not a white ministry; this is a
God ministry! I'm a part of this, not because I'm black. I'm a
part of this because I discern that this is *God*, and where God
is moving, I'm gonna get some of it."[22]

All three black Promise Keepers speakers, Garlington,
Evans, and Boone, acknowledge that both whites and nonwhites must take action to bring about racial reconciliation.
In his message to the largely white Pittsburgh crowd, Joseph
Garlington offered a practical way to start easing tension between the races. Speaking about racial crimes in his community, Garlington said, "In our black community, there has
never been a single white drive-by [killing] . . . They have all
been black. If you remove all the problems that white folks do
to blacks, you're still going to have black on black crime. And
that is what black folks need to take responsibility for. And I
can't blame you [whites] for the high rate of unprotected sex,
and for the high rate of illegitimate childbirth in the black
community, but I can say to you, when you're standing in another group of people, and there are no black folks around,
and you hear the first beginnings of the 'nigger joke,' that
would be the point for you to say, 'I can't listen to that.' "[23]

Garlington challenged the men, saying that as a result of
their involvement with Promise Keepers they should have a

new attitude toward people who have a different ethnic background than their own. As white men linked arms with black, Hispanic, and Asian men, Garlington encouraged them to promise, "When I leave here, I am going to be different. I'm not going to be disloyal, but I am going to stand with you whether you are present or not. And if it means losing a friend, because I now have a brother, I will lose that friend."[24]

Promise Keepers demonstrates racial equality and racial reconciliation by having men of color fill at least half of the keynote speaking slots at most of its public conferences. The chairman of the Promise Keepers board of directors is a man of color, Bishop Phillip H. Porter, Senior Pastor of All Nations Pentecostal Center in Aurora, Colorado. Bishop Porter brings with him a wealth of experience in racial reconciliation, having been involved in civil rights organizations for many years.

In another tangible step toward racial reconciliation, Promise Keepers pledged to contribute $1 million and countless man-hours, donated through local ministries, to help rebuild black churches that were destroyed in a spate of church burnings at the hands of arsonists in 1995 and 1996. Twenty-five percent of the Saturday afternoon offerings at both the 1996 Denver and Charlotte PK conferences was set aside to help restore the destroyed churches. Funds designated toward rebuilding the burnt-out churches began to be distributed in July 1996, the first check in the amount of $20,000 presented to Reverend Alfred Baldwin, pastor of First Missionary Baptist Church in Enid, Oklahoma. Together with other PK fundraising efforts, Promise Keepers raised $1.3 million in 1996 on behalf of the burned churches.

In a less public but perhaps more significant demonstration of Promise Keepers' commitment to racial reconciliation, PK is modeling its message in its hiring practices. According to *Christianity Today*, "Among PK's 437-member staff, 30 percent are minorities: 16 percent black, 13 percent Hispanic, and 1 percent are Asian. 'These numbers are unparalleled among evangelical organizations,' "[25] says Raleigh Washington, an African American and a Chicago inner-city pastor. In addition to his pastoral responsibilities, Washington has served as a member of Promise Keepers' board of directors and currently heads Promise Keepers' reconciliation division.

Nevertheless, in spite of Promise Keepers' desire for racial diversity at their conferences and their attempts to build bridges between the races, men of color for the most part continue to stay away from Promise Keepers events. In 1994, of the 278,600 men who attended PK stadium events, only 7 percent were nonwhite. That figure rose to about 10 percent of the more than 700,000 Promise Keepers attendees in 1995, and remained about the same in 1996. It's not that PK isn't trying to attract and facilitate men of color. During the pre-event publicity for the 1996 New York City conference at Shea Stadium, PK targeted men of color and particularly those of lower economic status more than at any previous conference. Despite PK's offer of thousands of freebies—free admissions worth sixty dollars, or "scholarships," in PK lingo—New York's men of color stayed away in droves. Men of color comprised only 25 percent of the crowd. Overall, the Shea conference was one of the most poorly attended, problematic, and expensive conferences of any that Promise Keepers has hosted to date.

I asked Raleigh Washington why more men of color were not showing up at PK events, especially since Promise Keepers was doing so much to make them welcome.

"We are seeing more men of color [showing up] but not in significant enough numbers that would make us say 'Wow!' " Washington replied. "There is a gradual increase, and we are now beginning to do some intentional things that are going to bring about even more of an increase."

Washington acknowledged that Promise Keepers plans to take a different tact in its efforts to reach men of color. "Promise Keepers did not do a lot of promoting in the white community," he admitted. "It got started by word of mouth, one man inviting another to attend a rally. But in the African American communities, for example, we must meet with the 'gate keepers,' those who are the influential pastors . . . then the men of color will respond better . . . In the Hispanic and the Afro-American communities, Promise Keepers is not likely to become a phenomenon unless the pastors are involved and say, 'This thing is right. Let's join it.' Because the pastor is still one of the most respected individuals in that community, even among those who do not attend church."

Raleigh Washington helped Promise Keepers design its four-point program of racial and sectarian reconciliation, which is included in the PK stadium syllabus. According to Washington, the principles of reconciliation require:

- A *commitment to relationship*, which means getting to know someone of a different race on more than a superficial level.
- *Intentionality*, doing something on purpose to make an effort in reaching out to someone of a different race. Suggestions include: "inviting a person of a different background to dinner in your home, visiting a church of a different ethnicity, or other activities that might stretch a person's comfort zone."
- *Sincerity* when trying to reach across racial lines. Washington suggests spending time together "to develop trust, being willing to be candid and honest, revealing hardships and weaknesses," and recognizing the ways walls can be built between the races.
- *Empowerment*, a PK term for spiritual renewal, re-

pentance, and forgiveness. "An attitude of repentance em-
powers the other person, group, or race to lay aside anger
and blame, and opens the path to forgiveness," says the
"Promise Keepers Statement on Biblical Reconciliation."[26]

Pastor Washington incorporates these same principles in
his multiethnic church in Chicago. He regularly leads discussion groups in his congregation, addressing head-on the
toughest issues that divide people of different ethnic backgrounds. The principles seem to be working, bringing people
of different races together who formerly have never brushed
shoulders.

While reaching the gate keepers to the nonwhite community
may be a key part of Promise Keepers' plan, many nonwhite
pastors are not as enthusiastic about Promise Keepers as Pastor Washington is. One pastor of an African American congregation said, "The needs of our people are so removed from
that of the average white congregation, they cannot even relate to us. I understand that, and I do not hold it against my
white brothers and sisters. I consider them genuine Christians. But the white guys who attend Promise Keepers cannot
empathize with me, and I really have no desire to empathize
with them."

A pastor of a largely Chinese congregation felt similarly. "I
am not opposed to anything that Promise Keepers is doing,"
he told me, "but I simply have no interest in becoming part of
the movement. Ours is a very close, family-type ministry, and
Promise Keepers' bigness is something that our people cannot
relate to when it comes to their faith. Many of our older members once worshiped in secret house churches in communist
China. Their children are accustomed to a small, intimate service, something a stadium meeting simply cannot provide."

Other pastors of nonwhite congregations see political and ideological differences in the multicultural leadership of Promise Keepers that cause them to shy away from PK. "Just because I am black does not mean that I am a social conservative, as are most of the Promise Keepers speakers," said one pastor. "Maybe if Promise Keepers would invite more of a balance between liberal and conservative men of color to speak from their platforms, it would create greater dialogue between the various groups."

Similarly, many white men who attend Promise Keepers events are not exactly overjoyed with PK's emphasis upon racial reconciliation. "They're hitting it too hard," said Samuel, a fast-food restaurant manager. "I'm just trying to repair my marriage and learn how to be a better father, and these guys want to dump all this guilt on me for racial sins of the past. I don't have the time or the energy for that."

Despite opposition and criticism, McCartney and his Promise Keeping troops are continuing to break down walls of racial bitterness and separation. Is it for real? Wellington Boone exhorted the press to watch and see. "If we're the real thing, God will show us off. If not, you can show us up."[27]

E. Glenn Wagner believes that Promise Keepers' simple approach to racial reconciliation can change the country. Wagner writes, "One man building a relationship with another man across racial barriers, demonstrating the love and power of God, will impact a home, and that home will impact a community, and that community will impact a nation."[28]

Is Promise Keepers' emphasis upon racial reconciliation working?

In Pittsburgh, I arrived late for the Saturday morning sessions and had to park about a mile away from the stadium in a rather seedy neighborhood. In broad daylight, I walked briskly and warily from my car to Three Rivers Stadium. That evening, at the conclusion of the conference, I stayed to watch the Promise Keepers stack every chair and clean up every speck of paper and other debris from the stadium floor before leaving. So amazed was I at the Promise Keepers' obsession with leaving the stadium cleaner than they had found it, I hardly noticed that daylight was slipping away. Darkness had fallen by the time I left the stadium and walked back toward my car, by myself, through the less-than-desirable section of town.

In the middle of a row of walk-up apartments, I saw a group of black guys gathered around a few disheveled white guys sitting on some steps. I thought, *Uh-oh, this doesn't look good.* I thought seriously about crossing the street, but instead I decided to keep walking toward the group on the sidewalk. When I finally got near enough to hear them talking, I realized that the white guys were homeless, and the black guys were offering them some of their food and telling them about Jesus. I recognized the familiar Promise Keepers' wristbands the black guys were still wearing. I thought, *It may not change the world, and it may not last, but for at least one night, Promise Keepers is having an impact in Pittsburgh.*

CHAPTER 9

CHRISTIANS OPPOSED TO PROMISE KEEPERS

For the men who have attended Promise Keepers events, and for the women who support them, it is hard to imagine how anyone of the Christian faith could possibly be critical of Promise Keepers. After all, the organization is dedicated to making men better husbands, fathers, and citizens by following Jesus Christ. What's to criticize?

Plenty, according to some.

Criticism from within Christian ranks falls into three loosely defined categories: those who think the movement is too willing to work with a variety of faith groups (ecumenical); those who think the movement is too focused on converting men to Christianity (evangelistic); and those who think the movement is too energetic, offering men an artificial euphoria that cannot be maintained once they return to the local church—*if* they return at all.

Unlike women's groups who criticize Promise Keepers for being too exclusive, those who believe that Promise Keepers is too ecumenical are worried that PK is too *inclusive*. The critics are concerned that Promise Keepers embraces men of all denominations—Baptists, Pentecostals, Methodists, Catholics, Presbyterians, Lutherans, Independents. PK even encourages men of other faiths—or of no faith—to attend its conferences.

Usually the critics of Promise Keepers' inclusiveness can be found on the far right fringes of evangelical Christianity, a group often labeled "Christian fundamentalists." These are not to be confused with most mainstream conservative Christians, who are often wrongly broad-brushed as "fundamentalists" by the media but are more accurately called conservative evangelicals.

The fundamentalists truly are the extreme conservatives of Christianity. They deplore the wide diversity of speakers employed by Promise Keepers, including such respected Christian leaders as Charles R. Swindoll, president of Dallas Theological Seminary; Bill Bright, director of Campus Crusade for Christ; E. V. Hill, African American pastor of Mount Zion Church in Los Angeles and one of the planners of Martin Luther King's famous 1963 March on Washington; Luis Palau, international evangelist; Joseph Stowell, president of Moody Bible Institute; and Bill Hybels, pastor of Willow Creek Community Church near Chicago, one of the largest Protestant churches in America.

The fundamentalists do not have nearly the platform or influence of the mainstream Christian men listed above, but they attempt to make up for their disadvantage, it seems, through voluminous writings and vehement opposition to evangelicals they consider to be compromising the Gospel's message. In the article "The Seven False Premises of Promise Keepers," Jack Stephens, a pastor from Columbus, Ohio, and an outspoken opponent of Promise Keepers, declares, "No fundamentalist in his right mind would ever associate with the hodgepodge of men and ministries involved with PK."[1]

Stephens particularly disdains the fact that many leaders of Promise Keepers are associated with charismatic churches that practice speaking in tongues and expect supernatural signs and wonders as part of their faith. Both Promise Keepers' founder Bill McCartney and PK president Randy Phillips have been affiliated with the Boulder Valley Vineyard, a charismatic congregation pastored by James Ryle, a member of Promise Keepers' board of directors.

Similarly, Stephens is offended that PK has openly welcomed Roman Catholics to participate. He and his fundamentalist colleagues would not agree that the Roman Catholic Church is simply another denomination, akin to Baptists, Methodists, and Assemblies of God. Because of their use of icons and statues (idols, the fundamentalists say), prayers to Mary (the mother of Jesus) and the saints, and an emphasis upon salvation through the church, Catholics are considered by the fundamentalists to be preaching false doctrine. A new breed of charismatic Catholics springing up within the church complicates matters even further. Says Stephens, "Catholics are still one of our mission fields. We can never reconcile with the false gospel of Romanism."[2]

Despite Bill McCartney's disagreement with Roman Catholics on some matters of belief, his desire to bring Catholics into the Promise Keepers fold is understandable. McCartney himself is a former member of a Catholic church. At one of the first Promise Keepers conferences, in an effort to emphasize the oneness of the men who had gathered regardless of denominational affiliation, Bill McCartney shouted, "Promise Keepers doesn't care if you're a Baptist. Are you born in the Spirit of God? Promise Keepers doesn't care if you're Pentecostal. Are you born in the Spirit? Now, hear me, Promise Keepers doesn't care if you're Roman Catholic. Are you born into the Spirit of God?"[3] This, to Pastor Stephens and others at his end of the Christian spectrum, is a clear sign that Promise Keepers is more concerned with having a worldwide ecumenical influence than it is about "pure doctrine."

But Promise Keepers generally have a broader view. One PK official seems to sum up the attitude toward Catholics in this way: "We have more areas in common with Catholics than we have areas in which we differ. The Catholic Bible has the same message of Jesus Christ—'You must be born again,' and 'Believe on the Lord Jesus Christ and you will be saved.' Sure, many in Promise Keepers have differences with the finer points of Catholic theology, but we choose to lay the emphasis upon those things on which we can agree."

And it is not just an embrace of Catholicism that troubles fundamentalists. David W. Cloud, editor of *O Timothy*, a fringe monthly magazine published by Way of Life Literature in Oak Harbor, Washington, writes:

> We are afraid of Promise Keepers. It will do more to build the harlot church of Revelation 17 than it will to build New Testament churches. The men who are reached through this ministry will not be brought into sound New Testament . . . churches and grounded in the truth. They will not be taught to keep themselves pure from apostasy and heresy. They will not be trained in discerning false gospels from the true. Rather they will be instructed in unscriptural ecumenism; they will be taught that doctrine is not crucial, that to fight for the truth is unspiritual. They will be encouraged to accept even apostate denominations as genuine expressions of Christianity. We know this is true because of the leaders involved in promoting Promise Keepers. Few men are more radically ecumenical than James Dobson [of Focus on the Family] and Stephen Strang

[publisher of *Charisma*, a magazine for charismatics, and *New Man*, the officially endorsed magazine for Promise Keepers]. Both accept Roman Catholicism as genuine Christianity.

Those who get involved with Promise Keepers will also be trained in a blasphemous mixture of humanistic psychology and corrupt Christianity. The presence of psychologist James Dobson within this movement guarantees this.[4]

As further evidence that Promise Keepers is too ecumenical, L. K. Landis, pastor of Fellowship Baptist Church in Liberal, Kansas, expressed concern that Promise Keepers encourages use of modern translations of the Bible. Every attendee of a stadium event is given a New International Version of the New Testament with the cover title "Man of His Word," published by the International Bible Society. Most Christians would see that as a good thing, but not Dr. Landis. He writes:

> The very ecumenical nature of PK demands an acceptance of the modern versions [of the Bible] and the corrupt texts from which those versions are taken . . . If a pastor sends (or worse, takes) his men to Promise Keepers then he is guilty of leading his men into unholy alliances with modernists, cultists, heretics, Bible-deniers and apostates.[5]

One group, the Independent Baptist Fellowship of North America, at its annual conference in 1995, passed a resolution condemning Promise Keepers. After listing several reasons for its actions, including PK's supposed ignorance of biblical doctrine and adherence to "psycho heresy," the resolution stated, "We therefore resolve and do hereby encourage pastors and laymen to take a clear stand and reject any participation with Promise Keepers lest God's command against compromise be dishonored and churches succumb to ecumenism . . ."[6]

In a scathing article listing reasons why Independent Baptists should not be involved with Promise Keepers, Dr. L. K. Landis concludes:

> It is our conviction that the Promise Keepers movement is a stench in the nostrils of God. It lends credibility to soul-damning cults [because of PK's willingness to welcome Jehovah's Witnesses and Mormons at its conferences]. It is led by Bible-deniers, haters of the truth and heretics. And participants in their meetings and rallies are guilty of being yoked together with unbelievers. God have mercy on that unfaithful shepherd [pastor] who willingly leads his men to the slaughter among the wolves of the Promise Keepers organization.[7]

Understand, the opinions of these fundamentalists are shared by very few in the broader spectrum of Christian churches and fellowships. No doubt the fundamentalists' scathing criticisms of Promise Keepers must sting the leadership of PK, especially since these groups are ostensibly fellow believers. On the other hand, Promise Keepers can take consolation in the fact that these same groups have consistently opposed another stadium-packing preacher . . . Billy Graham.

Many in more mainstream groups are nonetheless concerned about Promise Keepers' commitment to breaking down the walls between denominations. Jim Burton is a leader in "the Brotherhood Commission," the group helping to shape the men's ministries of the Southern Baptist Convention, the largest Protestant denomination in the United States, with fifteen million members. Although the Southern Baptists have endorsed Promise Keepers, and have even collaborated with PK to help design programs and materials for the denomination's various men's ministries, Burton expressed concern that when Bill McCartney and Promise Keepers vow to oppose racism and denominationalism, the impression is frequently given that the two targets are equally destructive. Some, particularly within denominations with very distinct identities or beliefs, chafe at that. Citing McCartney's comments in a 1995 interview with the *Arizona Republic*—"You will see Promise Keepers whacking away at those two giants like you've never seen before"—Burton admits, "Statements like this are very confusing to us." Acknowledging that McCartney probably intended to decry the petty divisions that separate denominations, Burton still worries that the impression is given that denominational distinctives have no place. "We try not to be defensive, but it's hard to digest that," Burton said.[8]

Similarly, the Lutheran Church Missouri Synod has issued an eleven-page study of Promise Keepers that encourages its members to attend PK events, while at the same time cautions them about the ecumenical aspects of Promise Keepers. The study questions PK's "propensity toward ecclesiastical unity based on dynamics other than a common faith confessed."[9] In other words, the concern is that Promise Keepers' open door, "y'all come" attitude may bring men into a common location but not necessarily into a common faith.

Despite the concern that Promise Keepers might blur individual denominational distinctions, most major U.S. denominations have adopted a "wait and see" approach to PK. "As long as they don't start encouraging men to move from one denomination to another," said a leader in a more liberal denomination, "we will not oppose their activities. But if we begin to see our men shifting their loyalties to some other church, we will sound the alarm."

Just such a concern has spawned a second group of PK critics, those who worry that the organization might be too evangelistic, seeking to make born-again, nondenominational charismatics out of everyone who becomes involved with Promise Keepers. "In our church, we do not emphasize crisis experiences with God," said one pastor who is troubled with PK's evangelistic approach. "We encourage our people to 'grow' a relationship with God. Consequently, we regard public responses such as those frequently called for at Promise Keepers as little more than antiquated means of eliciting an emotion-based reaction. Nevertheless, when men do in fact respond to the various invitations at Promise Keepers conferences, a strong bond is formed between them and the organization. I do not mean to say that Promise Keepers manipulates that bond to its own advantage, but they do ask the men to sign response cards, so PK can keep in contact with them after the event concludes. It is not a great stretch, then, to imagine men becoming more loyal to Promise Keepers than to their own church."

Promise Keepers consistently downplays such allegiances and attempts to redirect the men who are converted through its programs to a local church environment. As part of PK's effort toward racial and denominational unity, it is attempting to form partnerships with at least six denominations, including the Assemblies of God, the Church of God (headquartered in Cleveland, Tennessee), the International Pentecostal Holiness Church, the Southern Baptist Convention, and the Christian and Missionary Alliance. "We're trying to show denominations we're not their enemy," says Steve Chavis.[10]

Some critics of Promise Keepers' evangelistic overtones

have a philosophical problem; others see PK's evangelism as antithetical to their primary mission. "Privately, we are much more concerned with social issues than we are with evangelism," said a mainline denominational leader. "We have little interest in evangelism. Publicly, we would rather focus our attention on AIDS awareness, welfare for the poor, equal housing opportunities, school curriculums, and things of that nature. We are reluctant to involve ourselves with Promise Keepers because of Mr. McCartney's anti-choice positions concerning abortion and his homophobia. Our fear is that Promise Keepers' evangelism will recruit more of the same."

Kevin, a lay leader within the United Methodist Church, expressed a grudging appreciation of Promise Keepers' efforts to convert men to Christianity, but said, "Comparing our denomination's evangelistic efforts to those of Promise Keepers would be like comparing the difference in being kissed and being punched in the mouth. Both get a response but one is a lot easier to take."

Still other church leaders worry that Promise Keepers' overt evangelistic efforts and charismatic flavor will be used by groups more in harmony with PK's style in order to win men from one denomination to another. Recognizing that Promise Keepers' teachings could create such problems for its priests and parishioners, the Catholic Church has authorized several studies of PK, on both the local and national levels.

The Tidings, the official voice of the Roman Catholic Archdiocese of Los Angeles, reported on Father Christian Van Liefde's study of the feasibility and appropriateness of utilizing Promise Keepers at the parish level. "While noting the evangelical roots of the program, Father Van Liefde says there is no doctrinal issue which should cause concern to the Catholic Church.

" 'Promise Keepers places a very strong emphasis on returning to your own church congregation or parish and becoming an active layman,' Father Van Liefde points out. 'There is no attempt at proselytizing or drawing men away from their faith to another church.' "[11]

In June 1996, the U.S. Catholic Bishops' Committee on Marriage and Family issued an informational report on Promise Keepers that listed both the negatives and the positives of the organization from the Catholic Church's perspective. The negatives included lack of official Catholic presence at Promise Keepers events, lack of theological clarity about the balance of power between husbands and wives, and a concern that involvement in PK could cause some Catholic men to become Protestants. Other Catholics are troubled by rumors that Promise Keepers teaches "prejudice and discrimination against homosexuals" and "male headship," the idea that husbands are to exercise authority over their wives—concerns voiced by many mainline denominational leaders, as well.

On the positive side of the ledger, "Promise Keepers reignites in men an awareness of the spiritual dimension in life and offers them a safe place in which to find support and encouragement for Christian values and virtues," said Rick McCord, a member of the Catholic Bishops' staff.[12] McCord also said that many of the Catholic men who attend PK events return home to become more active in men's groups within their own parishes. McCord admitted, "There has been more activity in dioceses and parishes in terms of reaching out to men through small groups and other programs that hasn't been there before. Usually Promise Keepers is the trigger event."[13] For example, one new group within the Catholic Church that has been inspired by Promise Keepers is the CatholicMen Fellowships, which emphasizes the responsibility of men to society and their families, and stresses the spiritual side of men's lives. Two other national Catholic laymen's groups credit Promise Keepers as the catalyst that sparked their inception: Saint Joseph's Covenant Keepers, which focuses on small groups, similar to PK's accountability groups; and Ministry to Black Catholic Men, a group emphasizing a man's responsibility to his family and community.

Clearly, with its outstanding programming, huge numbers of participants, and high-energy enthusiasm, Promise Keepers could easily outshine most local or denominational men's groups, in spite of its stated desire to do the opposite. Some critics worry that such a phenomenon is already occurring.

The third group of critics expresses concern that the high-energy program and the overpowering euphoria of a Promise Keepers event is impossible to compete with, or to maintain, once the guys return home. A subtle fear is that after listening to some of the finest musicians and most dynamic speakers available in Christianity at large, as well as worshiping among tens of thousands of enthusiastic men, somehow the local church services are going to seem a bit ho-hum to men who have attended Promise Keepers. Some lackluster preachers and local church programs may see their formerly faithful men slipping off to more exciting venues. Prior to their Promise Keepers experience, the men may have been inactive, and half asleep, but at least they were *there*. Now that the spark has been lit, the local congregation does not always know how to contain the fire.

"We can't compete with all the fun and fanfare of a Promise Keepers conference," lamented a Connecticut local men's group leader. "Besides, some of the things that are considered appropriate in a stadium context don't always work well in the sanctuary. Some of the guys who came back from the New York City PK event wanted to clap their hands during the singing of the anthems. Other guys wanted to start calling out, 'We love Jesus, yes we do; we love Jesus, how about you?' right in the middle of our informal greeting-time after the morning offering. Those shenanigans were not well received by many in our congregation who have not experienced Promise Keepers' enthusiasm, nor do they care to."

The sense of camaraderie men experience at Promise Keepers is also difficult to maintain on the home front. "At Promise Keepers the men spill their guts with each other," observed Peter, an adult Sunday school teacher. "Then, when they come back home, some of them are embarrassed at their disclosures. It is not so easy to reveal one's worst fears and failures when you know you are going to see those same guys at the car wash or at your daughter's piano recital. Personally, I think Promise Keepers is setting these guys up for a big fall. At the same time, they are setting themselves up as an alternative to the church. The guys come home thinking, 'Who needs the church when we have PK?' "

Such fears are often unfounded, according to Douglas De-Celle, a Presbyterian pastor from Dayton, Ohio. Writing in the mainline Protestant magazine *Christian Century,* DeCelle reported that he found several things to quibble about, but few real concerns after spending time with the Promise Keepers at the 1996 Clergy Conference. Reverend DeCelle did not find any evidence that Promise Keepers is attempting to circumvent the local pastor or working to supplant the authority of the local church. Quite the contrary, he wrote, "The Promise Keepers' vision of renewal is that it begins in the pastor's heart and spreads to [the] congregation and beyond."[14]

He noted that it was easier to be critical of the meeting in the Georgia Dome, since no women pastors were in attendance and none were invited. Reverend DeCelle also rejected the contrived elements of the rally—"Everybody lift your hands!" or "We're going to get down on our knees"—and chose not to participate in those aspects of the conference, yet he nevertheless came away deeply moved. He particularly enjoyed the "exuberance" of the event, especially the singing on the first night when forty-two thousand male pastors were accompanied by the Atlanta Symphony.

On the broader issues of denominational and racial reconciliation, DeCelle was impressed by what he saw. "The Promise Keepers movement cherishes a passionate vision of interdenominational reconciliation . . . The problem is mistrust and criticism of one faith group by another . . . PK also envisions racial reconciliation. This is not simply a tangential theme meant to curry favor from liberal groups. Again, I was struck by the ardor: Breaking down walls is this movement's great passion. True to PK form, the pattern for reconciliation is to locate racism within oneself and then personally apologize to a representative of another race."[15]

Similarly, DeCelle dispelled the notion that Promise Keepers was teaching men to become dictators in their families. "My hunch is that, overall, PK emphasizes the husband's service to wife over family leadership . . . I realize that some feminist groups regard PK nervously, assuming that a movement of men can be nothing but reactionary. They see PK as striving to roll back women's hard-won progress over the past 30 years. Maybe I'm not subtle enough to detect how this might be operating. And I'm sure that some enthusiasts believe that Promise Keepers wants to turn back the clock. But I detected nothing reactionary, and in conversations with PK wives, I found no concern and often enthusiasm."[16]

Despite Reverend DeCelle's initial discomfort with Promise Keepers, he admitted that PK had inspired him to return to his pastoral duties with more vigor. "For me, the most poignant reaction to the experience came from a United Methodist district superintendent. During one of the breaks he stayed in his seat just shaking his head. He kept muttering, 'This is what we used to be like. John Wesley would love this.' "[17]

Some critics of Promise Keepers within Christian circles see cause for concern in PK's emphasis on accountability to other men. They say that only bona fide spiritual elders, such as priests, pastors, and bishops, can hold men accountable before God. More disconcerting to others is Promise Keepers' stress upon a man's total vulnerability and full disclosure to his accountability partners.

This type of relationship, critics suggest, frequently deteriorates when an accountability figure moves beyond a simple advisory role, demanding to be consulted on personal issues such as marriage, finances, when or if one should purchase a new home, whether to move to a new location, and a raft of other personal matters. The "discipling" or "shepherding" controversy erupted within many Christian charismatic churches in the 1970s. The movement was castigated for allowing pastors and other spiritual leaders to exert too much control over the personal lives of their followers, and it was soundly condemned by most Christian organizations and many high-profile Christian leaders. The same charge is sometimes brought against Promise Keepers because of its insistence that its men pledge to keep the Seven Promises and submit themselves to a group of accountability partners—not less than three men, not more than five, is often suggested as the optimum size for an accountability group.

Most men who have been involved with Promise Keepers scoff at the notion that PK is exerting too much influence in their lives. They point to Promise Keepers' commitment to helping pastors and local churches as evidence that PK wants to remain in a support mode. The criticisms of Promise Keepers from within the church, they maintain, come primarily from those who are concerned that they may lose their power or financial base as PK takes the spotlight off the local churches.

Indeed, although subtle and rarely spoken, the fear that Promise Keepers may siphon money away from the local church is nonetheless real. Pete, the pastor of a small congregation in Alabama, confided in me, "It makes sense that some of the guys who attend PK functions are going to send money to the organization. PK, with its huge stadium affairs and its thousands of men singing and clapping their hands, is after all much more exciting than our tiny congregation gathered in our backwoods church. Many of our men spend hard-earned money to attend Promise Keepers conferences and to purchase PK books and other materials, and that's fine. I don't mean to sound selfish, but what concerns me—and I don't dare say this to any of my men who have attended Promise Keepers—is that they will eventually start giving Promise Keepers money that should be designated to support our local church. PK sends out regular fund-raising letters, asking its constituents to send the organization money. I don't deny that Promise Keepers needs the money; nor do I deny that they are doing a great work. But I worry that if enough money flows out of our men's pockets to PK, sooner or later they will begin slacking off in giving to the church. The pie can only be sliced so many ways before somebody doesn't get any."

As for Promise Keepers itself, its leaders are continuing to encourage men to return to their local churches, to become involved in a small group with other men, and to make a difference in their community. PK also encourages men to "tithe"—to give at least 10 percent of their earnings to the local church—before sending any money to Promise Keepers. PK's attitude toward the local church seems to be: "We're in this together, so let's help each other."

At PK's 1996 Clergy Conference, Randy Phillips reminded the pastors of the incredibly short time it took to construct the Pentagon in Washington, a typically four-year project that was completed in eighteen months. Picking up on that idea as he addressed the topic of Christian unity, Max Lucado—pastor of Oak Hills Church of Christ in San Antonio, radio preacher, and bestselling author—told the crowd that in 1941 President Franklin D. Roosevelt convinced the United States Congress to commission the construction of the Pentagon because it was a special time. "It was a unique era, it was a pivotal point in the history of mankind," said Lucado.

Then Lucado suggested that Christians may be facing a similar time today. If so, he opined, several searching questions merit consideration: "Could it be that now God is again calling us to come under one roof? Could it be that right now, God is saying, 'This is the hour' . . . ?"[18]

It is one thing to dream about such common purpose when looking at denominational differences. But it is precisely that dream—all those Promise Keepers ostensibly under one umbrella, one political umbrella—that is causing some PK watchers to worry.

CHAPTER 10

PROMISE KEEPERS
AND REPUBLICANS

How do Promise Keepers vote? That question concerns many observers of the new men's movement. And perhaps with good cause.

A full quarter of all registered voters in the United States are white Protestants, according to a recent study by the Pew Research Center for the People and the Press.[1] Most Promise Keepers are—guess what?—white, married Protestants with above-average educations and incomes. It is easy to surmise that Promise Keepers is therefore not only becoming one of the most powerful religious forces in America today, but also rapidly cementing one of the most powerful voting blocks in American politics. Any organization that doubles in attendance and budget almost every year bears watching for its impact on society.

And Promise Keepers exercises influence beyond the obvious, heavily attended stadium events. PK sponsors scores of smaller, less-publicized events known as "wake-up calls" to alert the faithful concerning an ensuing large event, and to provide the uninitiated men in the smaller crowds a taste of

Promise Keepers enthusiasm that might whet their appetites for greater participation. To help pastors and men's ministry leaders "learn how to encourage and instruct men in shaping their convictions and upholding the Seven Promises in their personal lives," Promise Keepers also offers "Building Men of Integrity" seminars.[2] These advanced sessions were held in at least seven cities in 1996. In all, according to PK sources, more than 450 local and regional seminars, training sessions, and "wake-up calls" were conducted in 1996, landing a PK presence in all fifty states and seven Canadian provinces. Of course, to date, Promise Keepers' most outstanding feat must be the 1996 Clergy Conference, where according to PK figures 39,024 pastors—the largest gathering of Christian ministers in history—gathered for three days of PK's influence. Furthermore, in many of the twenty-two cities in which stadium events were held in 1996, a four-hour "Pastors and Worship Leaders" gathering was held, open to all men on the local church staffs.

Because of the large number of men (and women) involved with Promise Keepers, and the financial resources at its disposal, it is only a matter of time, political observers say, before the Religious Right jumps on the PK bandwagon. Many who have scrutinized Promise Keepers are convinced that the religious right has already done so, and is, in fact, the horse pulling the cart. They see Promise Keepers' commitment to Promise Seven—to influence the world—as a plot to inculcate the electorate with not only Christian values, but conservative political ideology, as well.

Critics also see political implications in Promise Keepers' attempt to establish a "key man" in each of America's 400,000 churches. The key man works in conjunction with the local pastor within the church to facilitate the small group programs deemed so essential by Promise Keepers. Of course, part of the key man's responsibilities will be to inform the other men in the church about PK news, providing a direct line of information between PK leadership to the church members. To help the key men, Promise Keepers has put in place about three thousand "ambassadors" stationed across the country. Both the key man and ambassador positions must be applied for through PK's national headquarters. These unpaid volunteers—13,842 men were serving as key men or ambassadors as of 1995—then work closely with Promise Keepers' forty state offices in an elaborate information network.

The organization has even gone high-tech. Promise Keepers has established PK NET, its own World Wide Web site on the Internet, providing a sophisticated, frequently updated flow of information to its followers. The PK NET includes the latest news on upcoming Promise Keepers events, testimonies of men (and women) whose lives have been positively affected by PK, and even "chat rooms" for those who wish to discuss the finer points of promise keeping.

None of these organizational lines of communication represent anything other than PK's desire to be on the cutting edge of the Information Age, but if Promise Keepers should choose to use its vast influence to affect the political process, either subtly or overtly, it has put in place the resources and the infrastructure to do so. Bill McCartney has never been bashful about expressing his own political opinions, especially on the matters of abortion and homosexuality, critics say, so why should it not be expected that McCartney and his troops will make bigger waves now that they have the ability to do so?

What worries political observers even more is Promise Keepers' intimate ties to conservative political figures such as former Republican presidential candidate Pat Robertson. Although Robertson has kept a much lower political profile since his failed bid for the Republican nomination in 1988, he continues to exert enormous influence among Christians through his television program, "The 700 Club," which airs on the Christian Broadcasting Network, which Robertson founded. Both Promise Keepers and Bill McCartney have received prominent and positive exposure on CBN.

Although Robertson has not been as visible in political circles, he is nonetheless extremely active behind the scenes through another organization he founded, the Christian Coalition, a political action group currently headed by Ralph Reed. The Christian Coalition is arguable the strongest conservative political action group in the United States today.

Some observers worry about more than Promise Keepers' chummy relationship with Pat Robertson. PK often takes shots for its association with Dr. James Dobson, Christian psychologist, popular radio program host, and head of the $100-million-per-year ministry Focus on the Family. Dobson, too, exerts great conservative social influence through a political lobbying and education group he founded, the Family Research Council headed by Gary Bauer in Washington, D.C. Although millions of people regard Dobson as a hero, those on the opposite end of the political spectrum frequently characterize him as "militantly antiabortion and antigay," depicting Dobson as evil and dangerous. To their alarm, Dobson is unequivocally pro-life, and is uncompromising in upholding the traditional nuclear family. He sees homosexual practice as a sin, a matter of one's choosing rather than simply a matter of genetics, upbringing, or environment, and this affects his stance on such issues as how employers and municipalities treat same-sex households and "domestic partners."

Promise Keepers' association with Dobson and Focus on the Family goes back to the early days of the PK organization.

Besides their headquarters' proximity in Colorado—Promise Keepers in Denver and Focus on the Family in Colorado Springs—Focus on the Family helped keep the fledgling Promise Keepers afloat until money from conference attendance began to pay the bills. Coach McCartney has been a guest on Dobson's radio show, and Dobson has been a keynote speaker for Promise Keepers. Focus on the Family's book-publishing arm also publishes some of the more popular books promoted by PK, including the controversial *Seven Promises of a Promise Keeper, Go the Distance,* and *The Power of a Promise Kept.*

Another high-profile conservative, Dr. Bill Bright of Campus Crusade for Christ, has been a Promise Keepers conference speaker, as well. Although he is not nearly as well known outside Christian circles as Pat Robertson and James Dobson, Bill Bright is familiar to millions of Christians for a simple booklet, "The Four Spiritual Laws," which offers basic instructions on how to find Christ. For nearly three decades, Dr. Bright has been an outspoken opponent of abortion and homosexuality. His more recent criticism of public education for teaching evolution without giving equal time to creationism, and his lobbying for a return of prayer to public schools, has once again brought him to the attention of those on the left of his political positions.

Many other Christian leaders who speak out on moral issues in the political arena have publicly endorsed Promise Keepers and have contributed articles to PK's books and magazines. Conservatives such as Jerry Falwell, who founded the Moral Majority; Dr. D. James Kennedy of Coral Ridge Ministries in Florida, who frequently uses his pulpit to address church-state issues; and former Nixon-administration staff member Chuck Colson, who served time in prison for his part in Watergate and now heads Prison Fellowship, a ministry for inmates, have all heartily endorsed Promise Keepers. No wonder, then, that while Promise Keepers adamantly protests that it is a nonpolitical group with no political agenda, those who do not share its conservative world view get nervous.

While Promises Keepers has remained mostly quiet on social issues (although it does provide position papers on issues such as homosexuality), the rhetoric on the left has been downright virulent. For instance, Suzanne Pharr, a self-described "lesbian leftie" and author of *Homophobia: A Weapon of Sexism*, wrote:

> I believe the Promise Keepers are the ground troops in an authoritarian movement that seeks to merge church and state. It does not matter that a rightwing agenda is not overt in the formative stages of this movement; when the leaders are ready to move their men in response to their agenda, they will have thousands disciplined to obey and command.[3]

Similarly, in an article by Nancy Novosad, Skip Porteous of the Institute for First Amendment Studies says of Promise Keepers, "They're building a list right now of 'godly politicians' to pray for."[4] In the same article, Porteous claims that his organization has been tracking Promise Keepers on a computer bulletin board. " 'It's almost totally political,' " he reported.[5]

Playing off Bill McCartney's statement, "By the year 2000, the strongest voice in America . . . is going to belong to the men of God," Nancy Novosad concluded her article by saying, "Promise Keepers says it plans to 'go the distance'—to impose its idea of leadership on the rest of the nation. By joining forces with the rest of the religious right, it plans to 'take America for Christ,' and to become the 'strongest voice in

America'—a voice that threatens a democratic, pluralistic society."[6]

Those who see PK as a religious branch of the Republican
party suspect that even Promise Keepers' much applauded
emphasis on breaking down the walls of racism is a political
ploy. An October 1996 article in *The Nation* warns dramatically, "If successful, the attempt to lure elements of minority
communities toward the right would complete the disman-
tling of the old New Deal Democratic coalition. While these
efforts have met with little success thus far . . . PK seems intent on creating and promoting a new urban religious leadership."[7]

Suzanne Pharr is even more blatant in expressing her
doubts of Promise Keepers' motives for calling an end to racism. She notes,

> Calls from the Christian Coalition and the Promise
> Keepers for racial reconciliation do not include any ef-
> fort to end institutional racism, or to stop coded attacks
> on "welfare mothers" or immigrants or affirmative ac-
> tion. Rather, moving into black churches gives the reli-
> gious right a foothold in the black community. In this
> way, the call for racial reconciliation is one of the most
> insidious aspects of the Promise Keepers and their al-
> lies on the Christian right. Just as the right is hungry for
> people of color who are willing to denounce affirmative
> action and the civil rights struggles that have tradition-
> ally benefited their communities, the Promise Keepers'
> recruitment of black church leaders looks like a way to
> persuade the black community to act against its own
> best interests.[8]

No one closely involved with Promise Keepers denies that
the organization is conservative when it comes to social is-

sues. But to contend that Promise Keepers is a shrewdly disguised vehicle for furthering the political agenda of the religious right—or of any group—is a jump that requires more of a leap of faith than that demonstrated by the men streaming to the front of the PK stages. It is an assumption steeped in preconceived notions that won't budge, no matter how often or in how many separate voices (or skin colors), Promise Keepers disavows having any political aspirations.

"It is a silly fabrication that reflects more of the liberal left's fears than reality," a PK leader told me when I presented him with some of the accusations that Promise Keepers was a Republican front. "To even suggest that our country has anything to fear from men becoming Promise Keepers is ludicrous. Sure, we want these guys to vote—that is part of being a good citizen—but we are out to change men's hearts, not their political persuasions."

For the most part, Promise Keepers chooses to ignore charges that it has political aspirations. In response to the flaming arrows fired from the liberal left, PK seems to be following the example of the One who advocated turning the other cheek, going quietly about doing good, even in the face of resistance.

And Promise Keepers speakers are cautioned before each conference to avoid hot-button issues on the platform. Occasionally an overzealous speaker will slip up and mention something PK would prefer that he didn't. For instance, E. V. Hill referred to the American Civil Liberties Union as "satanic" during his talk at the Los Angeles conference in 1995. While perhaps few men in the stadium—including the PK leadership—would have disagreed with Hill's statement, it was not the politically noncombative posture PK prefers.

In another example, PK speaker Greg Laurie seemed to take an indirect swipe at President Clinton during his talk at

Texas Stadium. Said Laurie, "When a man makes a promise to his wife—a marriage vow—and doesn't keep it, he is teaching her not to trust him." Laurie paused for effect before continuing, "And isn't it true that we have a problem like this with some of our leaders today?" The men in the stands responded with thunderous applause. When the noise finally died down, Laurie smiled mischievously and said, "I see some of you are ahead of me."[9] While the president was never named, few men in the stadium missed Laurie's point.

Even Chuck Colson, considered by many to be one of the more articulate living spokesmen for evangelical Christianity, seemed to raise the blood pressure of Promise Keepers' leadership recently when, speaking from the PK platform, he thanked a friend of his who was running for office, subtly implying an endorsement of the politician. Worse yet, as Colson began his speech following prolonged swells of applause and cheers, Colson slammed Congress, saying, "There is a proposal for welfare reform going on in Washington, D.C., right now. It is a bill called the Personal Responsibility Act. Now can you think of anything sillier than the Congress of the United States being able to pass a law and create personal responsibility? When you create personal responsibility, it's because men like you decide to keep their promises to God, and to their families, and to their country. That's what brings personal responsibility to America, not what the Congress does."[10] Colson's comments, though perfectly in character for him, were not considered appropriate by some PK leaders.

One factor causing critics to assume that Promise Keepers has designs on the White House, and state houses as well, is the prolific use of military and athletic imagery. "We're calling you to war," Bill McCartney told the crowd in Boulder in 1993. "We demolish arguments and every pretension that sets itself up against the knowledge of God, and we capture every thought to make it obedient to Christ." To the uninitiated, McCartney sounds like General Patton preparing the troops. What the Coach is actually doing is paraphrasing Scripture, specifically Paul's second letter to the church at Corinth, where the Apostle wrote, "For though we walk in the flesh, we do not war according to the flesh, for the weapons of our warfare are not of the flesh, but divinely powerful for the destruction of fortresses. We are destroying speculations and every lofty thing raised up against the knowledge of God, and we are taking every thought captive to the obedience of Christ" (2 Corinthians 10:3–5 NASB).

Granted, Promise Keepers talk a lot about warfare, but it is *spiritual* warfare they are discussing, the battle between Jesus and Satan, angels against demons, heaven and hell, life and death. And is anyone really surprised that a former football coach peppers his speeches with sports metaphors and says such things as, "We're gonna take back the nation for Christ"? When McCartney says, "We're calling men of God to battle—we will retreat no more," only people ignorant of Christian doctrine (or with their own agendas) would actually insist that the locker room–style pep talk is directed toward political or economic systems.

One can criticize the limits of such imagery, of course. "Bill McCartney comes from a football orientation, and the language Promise Keepers uses relies heavily on coaching metaphors and exhortations," says Rick Koepcke, a psychotherapist who counsels men in Thousand Oaks, California; "there's another whole part of the men's movement that emphasizes woundedness, brokenness, and the need for healing, but that side has pretty much been overshadowed by the emphasis on behavior."[11]

Certainly PK makes repeated use of military and sports imagery, but then, so does the Bible. Moreover, it is not merely accidental that Promise Keepers, dealing with men, meeting in a football stadium, emphasizing racial reconciliation, should draw heavily from the fields in which men are most racially integrated—professional athletics and the military.

McCartney told the pastors gathered in Atlanta, "Many of you feel that you have been in a war for a long time. Yet the fiercest fighting is just ahead. God has brought us here to prepare us. Let's proceed. It's wartime!"[12] Certainly such statements beg many questions. What war is McCartney talking about? What sort of fighting is imminent? And how is God preparing the men in attendance? But McCartney does not pretend to offer complex theological answers. He admits that he is not a biblical scholar or even a preacher. The man is a former football coach, not Billy Graham. Do he and other speakers at PK mix emotional hype with spiritual truth? Of course. Is it effective at motivating men to stand up for their faith? You bet.

And yes, McCartney enjoys referring to pastors as the "commissioned officers" in God's army. But then so did the Salvation Army one hundred years ago. Early Salvationists never talked about "sharing their faith"; they boldly declared that they had "fired a volley!" Yet along with being compelled to tell the world about their God, the early Salvation Army waged a war against hopelessness and despair . . . not to mention illiteracy, poverty, racial prejudice, drunkenness, and abuse. Rather than being a pawn of the religious right, might Promise Keepers be the heir of something more akin to the Salvation Army's passion to see society change, one person at a time?

To say that Promise Keepers "appears to be the 'third wave'

of the religious right, following the demise of Jerry Falwell's Moral Majority and the compromise of Pat Robertson's Christian Coalition with secular Republicanism"[13] is sheer presumption. Except for Promise Keepers' opposition to homosexuality and abortion, which is admittedly muted at that, it is difficult to understand how any observer trying to be objective could accuse the organization of being a political movement. The makeup of the men of Promise Keepers is simply too diverse; certainly many are Republican, but there are also many Democrats and Independents in the stadium crowds as well. And doubtless, some Promise Keepers are extremely active politically, but like many Christians, a large number of Promise Keepers are uninterested in the transitory political upheavals in Washington. They are much more interested in an eternal kingdom, one that will not pass away with the next election.

CHAPTER 11

PROMISE KEEPERS
AND THE WORLD

Imagine not seventy thousand men showing up for a Promise Keepers conference but seven hundred thousand! Does such an idea sound far-fetched? Not if you can picture Promise Keepers moving into South America and other countries where evangelicalism with a charismatic flavor is finding a warm reception. How well does Promise Keepers travel beyond the boundaries of the United States? Are men in other countries even interested in becoming Promise Keepers? The organization has a stated goal of changing the world, but what concepts can be exported to other countries without, on the one hand, compromising PK's message, or, on the other, imposing an uninvited, and often unwanted, doctrine upon people of other cultures? How much of Promise Keepers' message and methods will transfer to people of other faiths?

When I queried Steve Chavis of Promise Keepers, I was surprised at the straightforwardness of his answer.

"None," Chavis replied bluntly. "Sure, some observers

might say that the relational issues such as sexual purity, personal integrity, racial reconciliation, or respect for women will transfer, but Promise Keepers is about Jesus. If you are not interested in Jesus, sooner or later you will reject Promise Keepers."

Chavis's comments are echoed by the *Washington Post*. "This is not an interfaith effort, transferable to men of other religions," wrote Debbi Wilgoren. "Promise Keepers teaches that Christianity is the only truth. Its Christianity is conservative, holding that only men can be spiritual leaders, and abortion, homosexuality and sex outside marriage are always sinful."[1]

Nevertheless, Promise Keepers is compelled by the commitment stated plainly in Promise Seven to be obedient to Jesus' Great Commission. The Scriptural text upon which that commitment is based, Matthew 28:19–20, is included in every copy of the Seven Promises published by PK. Promise Keepers cannot be accused of concealing anything concerning its ultimate goals of worldwide influence. Few, however, actually take the time to look up Jesus' words behind the second part of Promise Seven. If they did, they might be surprised to discover that Jesus said: "Therefore go and make disciples of all nations, baptizing them in the name of the Father and of the Son and of the Holy Spirit, and teaching them to obey everything I have commanded you. And surely I am with you always, to the very end of the age" (Matthew 28:19–20 NIV).

Promise Keepers' international expansion is motivated by the same message that has catapulted multitudes of other missionary organizations across United States borders and around the world—to propagate not simply a message of maximized manhood, but of Jesus. Although this part of Promise

Seven has been given less public emphasis than other areas, going into foreign nations, making disciples, baptizing and teaching them are all part of one paramount goal—to have people enter into a relationship with Jesus Christ.

For most parts of the world, this necessitates conversion to Christianity, not simply a tacit acceptance of a Promise Keepers' "Let's be nice to everybody" public posture. In many countries, conversion to Christianity can be dangerous, costly, sometimes even deadly.

Whether other cultures are ready for them or not, Promise Keepers is going international. And the desire for them to do so seems in many places to be mutual. "We want Promise Keepers to come to Great Britain as soon as possible," said Ian, a blond wavy-haired young man from London. "Many Brits have had a fresh experience with God in recent years, thanks to a Billy Graham Crusade or other gospel outreaches. But we desperately need something that will bring British men out of the shadows and into the mainstream of Christian leadership once again."

Indeed, Promise Keepers has already begun expanding into several other countries. Representatives from three nations—Canada, Australia, and New Zealand—have been granted official status from Promise Keepers, and have already begun planning and holding conferences, leadership seminars, and other men-only events. The international PK organizations have their own separate legal jurisdictions, boards of directors, presidents, and management staffs, just as any multinational company might have.

"While these organizations are largely autonomous," states a PK publication, "each strictly adheres to Promise Keepers' Seven Promises, Mission Statement, and Statement of Faith. International offices are nonetheless culturally distinct entities, expected to build organizations tailored to local customs, ethnicity, and demographics."[2]

It is not exactly easy to win Promise Keepers' approval for an international franchise. Both to avoid the accusation that they are trying to impose their beliefs on other cultures, and because most American missions organizations long ago learned that foreign work must be indigenous to succeed, Promise Keepers wants the idea and the footwork for PK expansion to come from the country involved.

International representatives who want to establish a Promise Keepers organization in their own country must first form a group of "nationals" who will pray concerning the matter for at least six months. Besides time for prayer, the six-month period allows for a cooling of ardor that may be the result of attending a PK function in the United States. Sherry Kuehl, special assistant to Promise Keepers vice president of ministry advancement, explains, "It's important for them to be nationals—truly indigenous members of the culture. We ask them first to seek the Lord's vision for a minimum of six months. They might want to [organize a Promise Keepers affiliate], but it might not be the Lord's will or timing."[3]

The second step is for the foreign country's national organizational committee to prepare a "context paper" assessing the spiritual condition of the men in their nation, and the conditions of the local churches. According to Kuehl, their research includes such questions as, "Are their men's ministries already established? What do their churches look like? Are they 90 percent women?"[4]

Representatives from more than thirty countries have made official inquiries to Promise Keepers concerning the establishment of international PK organizations; twenty-two have already taken the initial steps required to become affiliated. By the middle of 1996, six countries were well on their way to satisfying Promise Keepers' initial requirements and were proceeding with plans to establish their own organizations. PK hopes to have the remainder of the twenty-two up and running by 1998.

One country close to being approved is South Africa. PK's Promise Six—seeking to bring reconciliation between races and denominations—could face a stiff test in that racially fragmented country, where the nation is divided predominantly between a majority of blacks and a minority of powerful, more affluent whites. Ron Pocock, a leader in what will become Promise Keepers South Africa, traveled to Denver in June 1996 along with representatives from three other nations to observe the PK national headquarters in operation, ask questions, and attend the PK conference in Mile High Stadium. Pocock anticipates a ready response in South Africa, despite the problems that nation has endured because of apartheid in the past. During his visit, Pocock said, "Just four weeks ago we had the leader of the respective 'white' and 'black' churches stand up in front of thousands on television, radio, and [in] newspaper[s], and declare that they sought forgiveness of one another. Reconciliation is happening in our country, and I believe Promise Keepers could be a major catalyst in bringing about the complete transformation."[5]

Like South Africans, many Canadians see Promise Keepers as a ray of hope when it comes to dissolving some of the racial tension between its people. The need for racial reconciliation in Canada takes a different twist. "The reconciliation issues in Canada focus more on native (Canadian Indian) versus non-native cultural populations," explained Bill Rutherford, president of Promise Keepers Canada, "not to mention those characterized by English-speaking versus French-speaking citizens. And one's cultural origin—Italian, Greek, French—often takes precedence. These walls are significant, even in the Church. We are praying that our common thread will one day be Jesus Christ."[6]

Rutherford's task is formidable: Canada has experienced heightened tension in recent years over Quebec's insistence upon being a separate entity from other provinces of Canada. Added to that, there is some truth to the stereotype that Canadian men are more staid, stoic, and isolated than American men. This, says Rutherford, may require a real difference in approach from that of PK in the States. "The Canadian definition of a man tends to be passive in providing leadership in the church and family, and often aggressive and self-sufficient in masculine identity. Our vision is that God will move in men's hearts, one man at a time, to get them plugged back into the church and into men's ministry, and assume an active leadership role in the family."

Rutherford's observation begs two questions: Will Canadian men *want* to reclaim leadership roles within the churches and families? And if so, how will the American Promise Keepers' emphasis upon men serving their mates play to the Canadian aggressive masculinity? Will Canadian men be able to express their aggressiveness by serving their wives and children? PK's response seems to be, "If American men can do it, Canadian guys can, too."

In existence only since 1995, Promise Keepers Canada is still trying to contextualize the resource materials, principles, mission, and values of its parent organization below the border. Rutherford readily acknowledges it may be slow going, but he sees enormous value in PK Canada developing its own identity. "We recognize the spiritual heritage of this call from the United States. But for this ministry to be all that God wants it to be, Canadian men need to take ownership."[7]

One of the things that Promise Keepers in other nations must face immediately is the vast difference in the number of men who attend their conferences compared to the numbers who show up at PK events in the United States. So far, the indigenous leaders are keeping things in perspective. Says David Emert of Sydney, Australia, "We had two [Promise Keepers] conferences in Australia this year. There were 550 men at one event. In Australia, that's fantastic! To have that many men praising the Lord in our country is very unusual. It's exciting to be in on the ground floor of God's work in our country."[8]

Clearly, though, the potential for massive PK stadium conferences exist within the international community, especially in South American countries such as Brazil and Colombia. Witness, for instance, the throngs of people who turned out to see and hear Pope John Paul II in 1996. Admittedly, it was a once-in-a-lifetime event for many members of the crowd, but the incredible response to the pontiff's visit shows that a spiritual hunger exists. It is therefore easy for avid Promise Keepers to envision a South American Promise Keepers conference that would dwarf anything yet done in the United States.

The potential of Promise Keepers in Europe is also a topic that excites many PK leaders, although most of them are reluctant to say so publicly. "Imagine, Catholics and Protestants gathering together in the same facility in Belfast," dreams one PK representative. "Better still, think what might happen if Promise Keepers could bring men together in the Middle East. Can you imagine a PK conference in Israel, in which both Israeli and Arab Christians gathered together? What might happen?"

Although I had difficulty sharing his almost naive enthusiasm, I had to admit that such dreams are contagious. After all, so many of the world's problems have religious roots, yet so few peacemakers consider the possibilities of bringing people together in a religious context. If Promise Keepers could help break down walls in the United States between Baptists and Pentecostals, Catholics and Protestants, might it have some measure of success in bridging the gaps between the international community? One can hope.

Admittedly, much of the PK message is exclusive. Victor Nazario, a Hispanic pastor in the heart of Harlem, was the New York City event manager for the 1996 Shea Stadium conference. On a daily basis, he struggles with making the Christian message palatable to the majority of black Muslims who surround his inner-city church. When I asked Pastor Nazario how he perceives Promise Keepers will be accepted in strongly Muslim areas, he tried to be positive but he could not ignore the abrasiveness of the Gospel of Jesus Christ. "Some of the Muslims in our community are very eager to mix with Christians and talk about Jesus," he said. "But the Jesus they are talking about is not the Lord Jesus Christ. They don't believe in the Christian understanding of Jesus. Not long ago, I sat down and spoke to a group of Muslims for about three hours. They didn't believe that Jesus died on the Cross. They didn't believe that Jesus is Lord and that he is God. If the Muslims feel that we are trying to convert their people, most of them will feel a threat, and they will be very active against it."

Despite certain opposition in some countries, Bill McCartney is committed to seeing Promise Keepers circle the globe. Coach McCartney sees the Gospel message, packaged in a Promise Keepers "container," as being inclusive—for all people, everywhere, transcending cultural barriers. In his November 1996 financial solicitation letter, Coach Mac exulted, "How exciting it is to see God's work through Promise Keepers spread beyond the borders of our own country! It is as

though the words from Isaiah 55:5 are speaking to PK—
'Behold you will call a nation you do not know and a nation
which knows you not will run to you, because the LORD your
God, [even] the Holy One of Israel; [for He] has glorified you' "
(NASB).

As though giving a rousing half-time talk to a team that
was ahead but not yet assured of victory, Coach McCartney
declared, "I don't want to stop this international expansion.
We don't want to keep God's Word from reaching men outside
America's borders!"[9]

Promise Keepers intends to approach the international
scene by using much of the same methods it has used so suc-
cessfully in the United States—establishing an extensive key-
man and ambassador network, for example, to disseminate
information to each local church and to work with the local
pastors. PK leadership has seminars and wake-up calls
planned in a variety of countries, although they may have to
use different terminology in some places. The plans include
mass rallies as well. All this emphasis upon strategy, however,
is new to PK. In the United States, the movement spread primarily through word of mouth. Little time, money, or man-
power was spent trying to figure out how to make it happen.
In the United States, Promise Keepers simply exploded.

As such, Promise Keepers must now grapple with how it
can best present a positive impression of the Gospel. According to one high-level PK source, Promise Keepers does not
want to repeat some of the mistakes other multinational ministries have made. "We want to love men into coming, not
condemn them for their sins and failures. The secret will be
prayer, just as it is in the PK conferences at home. Believe it
or not, it's easier to get American Christians to protest than it
is to pray, but we are convinced that nothing lasting will hap-

pen without concentrated prayer. That and building trusting, one-to-one relationships inside each country will be the key to our success."

"Or failure?" I suggested.

"Our success," the PK representative said with a smile.

CHAPTER 12

PROMISE KEEPERS AND YOU

Two couples—Mary Beth and Frank, and Tina and Gary—come from Christian family backgrounds. Both live in affluent neighborhoods. Both couples have been married about fifteen years—and both are on the verge of divorce.

Mary Beth and Frank have two boys, ages twelve and fourteen, a large Cape Cod home, and close to a six-figure income. Mary Beth is an outgoing, vivacious, involved-in-everything "soccer mom." She thrives on activity, and barely finishes one project when she starts another, whether it's volunteering at the family's church, the boys' school, or for the latest community cause. Frank, on the other hand, is a true introvert. He dislikes being with people other than his immediate family, and could easily spend his life sitting in his easy chair, reading a book, and indulging in his only known vice—smoking expensive cigars. Their marriage has not been horrendously bad; in fact, most people might have been fooled into thinking that they were a picture of midlife contentment. But in truth they were not content with each other; they were indifferent to each other. Mary Beth was obsessed with her activities; Frank did his job, came home, and read another book.

When Mary Beth heard that some men from their church were going to attend the 1996 Promise Keepers conference in Memphis, she immediately signed up Frank to go along. Frank stubbornly refused. "The last thing in my life that I want to do is spend a weekend with sixty thousand other men!" Frank said angrily when he learned that Mary Beth had preregistered him.

Mary Beth continued to hope and pray that Frank would change his mind. As the conference weekend drew nearer, she and several of her friends prayed specifically for Frank. She felt certain that the Promise Keepers conference was a "divine opportunity," a chance for Frank to experience God in a fresh way, and perhaps discover some formula for reclaiming life for their marriage.

To this day, neither Frank nor Mary Beth know what made Frank change his mind. Mary Beth did not nag him about going to Promise Keepers. She rarely even talked about it. When the registration material, admission wristband, and Promise Keepers music cassette arrived in the mail, she put it in the stack with all of Frank's other mail, without even drawing attention to it. She did mention that some of Frank's acquaintances—he had no close friends—were going to the Memphis event.

For whatever reason, Frank got up on the Friday morning of the conference, called in to work, and said he was taking the day off. He then phoned one of the fellows from church to ask what time the bus was leaving. The man's wife answered, "I'm sorry, Frank. We didn't think you were going. The bus left already."

Frank got in his car and drove to Memphis, about a five-hour trip. Once he arrived at the Liberty Bowl, he found his way into the stadium and sat down among men he had never before met. It was totally against Frank's nature to mix with strangers, but the men made him so welcome, he decided not to search for the more familiar men from his church. In fact, he never did hook up with the guys from his church. He stayed right there throughout the conference, soaking up every word, experiencing the odd sensation of being surrounded by thousands of bodies, yet feeling somehow as though he were the only guy in the stadium.

Frank did not respond to any of the invitations to go down front for prayer that weekend. He reluctantly joined with the other men around him when the various speakers encouraged the audience members to turn to three or four men nearby to pray, or to discuss a point that had been made. Frank was not interested in hearing the other men's prayers or their opinions. But something was happening to Frank on the inside nonetheless. He was being changed—imperceptibly—but changed.

When he arrived home, Mary Beth was waiting up for him. She and her friends had prayed again that God would do something special for Frank at Promise Keepers. When Frank supplied only his usual perfunctory responses to her excited questions, she was disappointed in Frank, disappointed in Promise Keepers, and disappointed with God.

But something about Frank *had* changed. He began to be more attentive to Mary Beth. He volunteered to go with her to many of her activities, without her having to ask him. He talked more, and not just about current events, but about his feelings. Most surprising, Frank occasionally asked Mary Beth about *her* feelings. He was still the same Frank, but he began to do little things that Mary Beth regarded as special acts of love—putting an extra blanket on her feet while she watched television at night, or feeding the cat, which she knew he hated. Over the next weeks and months, Mary Beth realized that she was living with a different man, a man who was trying to serve her.

Mary Beth began to reciprocate Frank's expressions of love and affection. She often touched his hand when she spoke to him. She made special meals that she knew he enjoyed. She made it almost a game to see if she could do more for her husband than he was doing for her. She began to read a bit more, too, nothing heavy at first, but more serious than the pulp novels and magazines she normally read. To her surprise, Frank seemed enthralled when one night she began to tell him about a book she was reading. They actually had a discussion that had nothing to do with the children, bills, church, or school. Although it has been only a matter of months since Frank attended the conference in Memphis, Mary Beth says emphatically, "Promise Keepers saved our marriage!"

Tina and Gary's marriage was floundering, too. They live in mid-state New York, and Gary was excited about attending the 1996 Promise Keepers conference at Syracuse. Gary knew that his relationship with Tina was going nowhere, and he honestly hoped that he could pick up some tips at the conference that would help him win Tina back. The couple had been struggling in their relationship for years and had nearly called it quits several times. Alcohol and sexual "flings" had taken a toll on their marriage in the past. Although the drinking had subsided and the affairs were over, trust in each other was virtually nonexistent between the couple. Only their faith in God, and concern for their teenage daughter, kept them from giving up on their marriage and filing for divorce.

At Promise Keepers, Gary entered into the stadium atmosphere wholeheartedly. He sang, he prayed, he spilled his guts

to the other guys in his group, asking them to pray for him—
pray that he would be a better husband and father and that
Tina would be able to see a difference in him. He practically
leaped to his feet when the opportunity was given to pledge
obedience to the Seven Promises. On the way home, in the
bus along with the other guys from his church, Gary dozed
contentedly. He couldn't wait to begin being a better servant
in his home, in his church, and in his community.

When Gary arrived at home, Tina was still awake, watching a movie in their basement den. Gary immediately began
telling her all the exciting things he had experienced at Promise Keepers, about the music, and the singing, and the guys
tossing Styrofoam airplanes and beachballs, and this speaker
said . . . and that speaker . . .

Tina couldn't have cared less.

She listened politely for a few minutes, then simply said,
"Sounds great, Gary," as she turned up the volume on her
movie.

Undaunted, Gary tried again. "Things are going to be different around here, Tina, just you wait and see. I'm going to
try to out-serve you."

"That shouldn't be hard," Tina replied coldly, as much to
herself as to Gary.

Gary stood in the middle of the room, looking at his wife.
He understood that they had been through some tough times,
but they were at least still together. Didn't that count for
something? Disappointed and dejected, Gary just shook his
head, and went upstairs to get ready for bed. "She'll see," he
said aloud.

For the next two months, Gary really did try to do everything he could to out-serve Tina. He bought her flowers for no
special reason. He washed her car, even on days when he
didn't have time to do his own. He cooked dinner on several

occasions, simply to help out around the house. Tina, however, remained unimpressed. And untouched. Gary and Tina are still married, but by all indications, their relationship has changed very little, despite Gary's attempts to stick to his promises. Gary has not given up, and hopes to start seeing a change in Tina anyday now.

What makes the difference? Why is the Promise Keepers experience so life-changing for some relationships, while for others it barely makes an impression? Who can say. Certainly intangible factors such as faith, a positive attitude, and a willingness to change are crucial. Accountability to people who care can help, but may not be as necessary as Promise Keepers suggests. Gary had an accountability group; Frank did not.

Perhaps the more pertinent question is: What can Promise Keepers do for you? Surely, in most cases, it must be said that involvement with Promise Keepers or at least the adoption of PK principles such as integrity, sexual purity, a willingness to serve one's spouse, children, and community, and the breaking down of walls that foster division and hatred can be a positive experience for almost anyone. In my research for this book, I was hard-pressed to find a few men or women who had actually had association with Promise Keepers and were convinced that they or their families were negatively affected as a result. I found some who disliked Promise Keepers for various reasons; I found many who disagreed with Promise Keepers' message or methods; but of the men who had attended PK events, the reports were overwhelmingly positive.

Surprisingly, the support of the wives of Promise Keepers was almost unanimous. A few women, whom I at first thought to be unhappy with their husbands' PK involvement, probably would have been upset no matter what organization took their husbands away for the weekend. Terri, a disgruntled wife of seven years, was typical. When I asked her what she thought of her husband's new commitments following a Promise Keepers conference, she laughed sarcastically. "Hmmph," she said, "if he wants to go out and change the world, he can start by going out to the garage and changing the lightbulb that's been burnt-out for the last two months."

But the Promise Keepers experience is replete with poignant stories of people who not long ago had no hope, but now have rekindled a relationship with someone from whom they were estranged—fathers and sons, husbands and wives, white men and men of color, men and God.

While much is made and appropriately so, of the renewing of commitments between husbands and wives as a result of Promise Keepers, the reconciliation between fathers and sons is equally impressive. Carl, for example, is a retired dentist, a Christian for years, and the father of a forty-two-year-old son, Don. In his early teens, Don rebelled against his father's rules and regulations, and most of all against Carl's religion. Carl constantly railed at his son, warning him that he was going to end up as a worthless piece of dung if he didn't get his life together, and especially if he didn't "find God."

Don didn't find God. He wasn't even looking for God. Quite the contrary, he wanted to get as far away from his father and his father's God as he could. At eighteen, Don enlisted in the Navy. For the next twenty years, Don literally circled the globe, sometimes stationed for months on nuclear submarines. He spent the last few years of his Navy career living in Hawaii, as far from the East Coast state in which his dad lived as Don could get while still living in the United States.

When he retired after twenty years of service, Don returned home to see his aging mother and father. It so happened that his dad was going to a Promise Keepers conference in Washington, D.C., that weekend. Don went along. As Don sat listening to one speaker after another talk about relationships, he began to think back to his early years. The thing he missed most in his life was the fact that he and his dad were never friends.

During the Saturday morning session on the subject, "Turning Your Heart Toward Your Children," Don realized what had turned his heart away from his dad. His father had hardly ever been home as Don was growing up. Carl was working constantly, trying to build a bigger and better dental practice, going on missionary trips with the church to help fix kids' teeth thousands of miles away, while Don had to wait for months at a time to get in to see his own dad for a checkup. Carl worked long hours, and when he came home, he was usually too tired to do anything special with Don. Any spare time the man had, he poured into church activities. No wonder Don rebelled against his dad and his dad's religion.

As Don sat wondering what to do with the realization of why he had resented his father all those years, the speaker on the platform was hammering away at the dads in the audience, encouraging them to be the fathers who are there for their kids. Suddenly, Don felt his father reach an arm around his shoulder—something Don could not recall him ever doing before—and leaning his face toward Don. Tears were trickling down Carl's face.

"Son, I'm sorry," Carl said aloud, but quietly. "I was there for everyone else while you were growing up, but I was never there for you, not when you needed me, anyhow. I'm so sorry. I can't change what's been done, but please forgive your old man, will ya?"

Don wanted to answer, but he couldn't. He wanted to shout, "You're right! You *weren't* there for me. *Never!*" But those words wouldn't come. To his own amazement, as the

PK speaker continued lecturing, Don heard himself say, "Okay, Dad. I forgive you."

A reservoir of tears seemed to burst inside him as Don, the rugged, retired Navy officer, began bawling, totally oblivious to everything and everyone else around him—except his dad. While the preacher preached on, a miracle of sorts was taking place in the bleachers as a father and son bonded in a way they had never done before.

Indeed, one of Promise Keepers' greatest contributions to society may not be the reconciliation of the races or denominations so much as it is the reestablishment of the father-son relationship. At any of the Promise Keepers stadium events, it is not unusual to see fathers and sons walking together. Often as many as four thousand teens accompany their dads to Promise Keepers conferences. Usually the fathers are in their mid-thirties to early forties, and the sons are twelve-to-fifteen years of age, but sometimes kids as young as eight and ten show up with their dads. Several of the PK conferences include a special Saturday morning "Youth Breakout Session," a two-hour segment in which the boys have their own Promise Keepers program in a separate room while their dads are hearing about how they can be better husbands and fathers. Then, around 11:30 A.M., in one of the most dramatic episodes of any Promise Keepers conference, the boys are reunited with their dads.

The boys stream back into the stadium, usually running to the front of the staging area. As the boys pour through every available entrance, the dads rise to their feet to greet them, giving their sons a standing ovation that sounds like a thousand Niagaras pouring down atop the kids. Minute after minute goes by, and still the dads are applauding their boys. It is doubtful that any father can witness such an event without tearing up, whether he has sons or daughters. Finally, when the platform speaker restores order and quiet, the dads pray for their sons and the sons pray for their dads.

Contrived? Sure. Manipulative? Maybe. But effective? You better believe it! Those boys will never forget the ovation they received from their dads in those stadiums, but more importantly, the celebration of fatherhood does something almost mystical in the hearts and minds of the dads. Said one father of four, "This reminds me what a tremendous privilege and responsibility it is to be a dad. Sometimes I get frustrated with my kids—like most parents do—but today I have been reminded that I am the best—or worst—Christian my boys are ever going to remember. I want to do it right. I want to be the kind of dad that my boys can look at and say, 'Yeah, now that's the kind of guy I want to be someday.' "

I witnessed another poignant Promise Keepers moment when I walked over to the wheelchair section at the Indianapolis RCA Dome conference. There, dozens of men confined to wheelchairs were singing along, praising God despite the fact that some of them could not raise their hands as the other men in the stadium were doing. None of them could stand—one guy lay prone on a stretcher—and some of the guys were unable to talk, much less sing. But all of them—in their own way, whatever way they could—were praising and thanking God, and committing themselves to being better men.

At one point, during a break in the speaking and singing, a "wave" was taking place throughout the stadium. Guys in one section after another leaped to their feet, threw their hands into the air and roared something about Jesus, then sat back down as the next section picked up the wave. Around and around the stadium the wave went, the volume of the roar increasing in decibels to where the inside of the RCA Dome sounded like the blare from hundreds of jet engines.

In the wheelchair section, the men struggled to participate.

Some raised their arms as the wave went by. Others tried to sit up a little higher in their chairs. Some could only raise their eyebrows when it was their turn to wave for Jesus. Everyone did something as an expression of praise. It was a sight I will never forget, but I could not stay in that section for long. It was simply too overwhelming.

Perhaps just as significant are the many "ordinary" families affected by Promise Keepers—husbands and wives who are not in crisis but who are nonetheless challenged to be better partners as a result of Promise Keepers. Michelle and Steve Carrington were such a couple. Avid golf fans, in January 1996 they had already made reservations and purchased their tickets to attend the PGA golf classic held at Kingsmill Resort in Williamsburg, Virginia, during a weekend in July. When Steve heard that the Promise Keepers conference was coming to Three Rivers Stadium in Pittsburgh, less than an hour from their home, he and Michelle were excited; when they learned that the event was to be held during the same dates as their vacation, their excitement turned to disappointment.

"Don't worry about it, Michelle," Steve told his wife. "I know how much you have been looking forward to going to the golf tournament in Williamsburg. There are lots of Promise Keepers conferences. The Indianapolis conference is coming up after Pittsburgh; maybe I can get to that one."

Michelle knew that if Steve missed the Pittsburgh event, he would not be able to attend Promise Keepers that year. His heavy work schedule would not allow him to take off anymore time that summer. Besides, she had been praying for her husband to have a closer relationship with God; maybe this Promise Keepers conference was the answer.

She told him, "No, Steve. You go to Promise Keepers. I'll cancel our reservations at Kingsmill." Michelle later said, "I felt that if Steve attended the Promise Keepers conference, it would be an investment for our whole family. There was no way that I wanted him to miss it."

She and Steve would still be somewhat together that weekend—it was their vacation, after all. Michelle signed up to work as a PK volunteer during the conference. She was assigned to the press box area, where she could not only see what her husband was experiencing, but hear the conference speakers as well.

The weekend had such a profound impact upon Steve that, when it was over, Michelle decided to sit down and write Promise Keepers a letter of appreciation, thanking them for their work with men, a gesture that, unknown to Michelle, thousands of other women have also made. In her letter (used by permission), Michelle told of her family's change in vacation plans, and then wrote:

> My husband went to the PK conference in Pittsburgh and he loved it! He has not been the same since. My husband has always been thoughtful of my needs and an excellent provider for us and I am very thankful for that. But now he is becoming the spiritual leader of our home. I am so grateful to Promise Keepers for their work and sacrifice.
>
> My husband now meets once a week with a small group of men in their respective homes. He also meets once a month with a larger group of men in our church. He loves both of those meetings and receives great encouragement from attending them.
>
> He has always been a good husband and a wonderful father, but thanks to his participation with Promise Keepers, he is even better!
>
> Also, I had the privilege of working as a volunteer in

the press box area. I saw the results of the moving of the Holy Spirit and I felt extremely humbled to be in the presence of God.

In my opinion, the PK conference was the most powerful, meaningful, and life-changing Christian conference I have ever attended. By the way, it was better than any vacation we ever had!

Jon and Marty Lauber own a sporting goods store in Elyria, Ohio. The Laubers were both Christians prior to Jon's involvement with Promise Keepers, but it was mostly Marty who led the way when it came to things spiritual. Jon wanted to be more outspoken about his faith, but had felt inadequate to express his feelings about God. God-talk just wasn't something guys did in his line of work. "Please don't ask me to pray or say anything in front of other people," Jon often said to Marty, "because I simply cannot do that."

Then, in 1994, at the urging of some relatives, Jon attended his first Promise Keepers conference. When he returned home, Marty could hardly believe the transformation that had taken place. Where before Jon felt he could not talk to anyone about God, now Jon could not keep quiet about his relationship with Christ. He volunteered to teach a Bible study; soon he became involved in the leadership of their church.

While Marty welcomed Jon's increased spiritual involvement, it was a mixed blessing. Jon became so excited about his faith that Marty almost became intimidated. Suddenly, people at their church were not asking Marty to speak or to take leadership roles. Now they were as likely to ask Jon as they were Marty. "At first, I didn't know if I liked that," Marty confesses. "I knew that I had some leadership qualities and yet I didn't want to impede what was happening to Jon. I tempered myself, though, and became involved in other Christian organizations outside of our church groups, so I could still have an outlet for my skills without feeling that Jon and I were in competition. That worked well for me. Sure, it meant a slight adjustment for me, but it was well worth it to see the change in Jon. Indirectly, I have benefited in marvelous ways because of Jon's PK commitments. Meanwhile, Jon has continued to grow stronger spiritually and more involved with Promise Keepers. The other day, he said, 'I think I'd like to become a PK ambassador.' I could not have even imagined Jon saying something like that just a short time ago. But if he decides to do it, I'll encourage him each step of the way."

While many women benefit from men attending Promise Keepers events, many communities are positively affected as well. For instance, when pastor Erick J. Adams accompanied several men from his congregation in Clymer, Pennsylvania, to the Pittsburgh conference, he told the men to expect to have their priorities challenged. They were.

When they returned to their rural community of about two thousand people, Pastor Adams's men were excited to put into practice what they had learned at Promise Keepers. One of the first things they did was to call the elderly members of the congregation and offer their assistance to do cleanup and repair work in the homes of the church's senior citizens. "Any work that you need done," the men told one retired couple, "we will see that it's completed at no charge to you."

Promise Keepers' emphasis upon practical Christianity is one of the most endearing aspects of the movement. At the RCA Dome, on Thursday—setup day—I was one of the last people to leave. Sitting in a room beneath the stands, I had enjoyed eating an evening meal with some of the PK staff members. It was a simple meal—pizza, salad, soda pop, and some pie for dessert—but my host had gone out of his way to make sure not only that all of the men and women working for PK were fed, but the stadium security staff and cleanup crew as well.

As people slipped away, one by one, I sat at a table and finished my meal by myself, waiting for my host to return. After a few minutes, two African American women sauntered into the area beneath the stadium. They looked to be in their mid-fifties and were dressed in work clothes, obviously part of the stadium cleanup crew.

One of the women looked around and shook her head. "I don't believe it!" she said.

Thinking that she was talking to me, I swallowed my mouthful of pie and said, "Excuse me?"

"I don't believe it," she said again. "I know these boys are Christians."

She had my attention now. "Really?" I asked. "How can you tell—by their hats?"

"No, honey," she said with a warm grin. "That's not how I can tell."

"Because of the slogans on their shirts?" I asked, pointing to a passing PK worker, just leaving. His T-shirt bore a slogan on the front: WHAT HAS JESUS DONE FOR YOU LATELY? On the back, it showed a drawing of a nail in Jesus' hand and the slogan HE STRETCHED OUT HIS ARMS AND DIED FOR YOU.

The cleaning woman shook her head. "Naw, that ain't it. Anybody can wear a shirt. That don't mean nothin'."

"Then how do you know these guys are Christians?" I asked, genuinely puzzled.

She pointed to the large garbage cans in the corner. Both of them were full. "I know they is Christians because they pick up their trash," the woman said matter-of-factly. "I clean here all the time, and honey, you don't want to even think 'bout some of the messes I've had to clean up. But not with these boys. Look at that floor. Not a napkin or a cup in sight. They've been picking up their trash all day, too. I know they's Christians. They pick up their trash."

One of the most intriguing people I met as I was doing the research for this book was not a Promise Keeper but a Promise Keeper's wife. Dottie Byrd and her husband, Richard, married young; she was twenty and Richard was nineteen. They settled in Hartville, Ohio, a small town near Akron. They had two children—a daughter, Natalie, and a son, Kyle. Richard took a job with Federal Express and the family became involved in a large local church in Akron. Dottie and Richard were active with a Bible study group and worked with the children's choir. An attractive couple, with two darling children, the Bryds seemed to have life all together.

In the spring of 1994, Dottie and Richard were busy with their family and church activities. They were also working as volunteers for an upcoming Billy Graham Crusade. Already a dedicated Christian, and consumed with getting ready for the Crusade, Richard was reluctant to take a weekend away from home to attend the "Seize the Moment" Promise Keepers conference at Indianapolis in June 1994. But eventually, with the coaxing of Dottie's brother-in-law, a pastor in Indiana, Richard decided to go.

One of the things that left an indelible impression upon Richard took place as the men exited the RCA Dome on their way to pick up their lunches at the noon mass-feeding on Saturday. As the men with whom Richard was walking came out of the stadium, they were singing the old hymn "Holy, Holy, Holy." They had to cross under the street through a tunnel, singing each step of the way, and as they did, the sound of the classic song reverberated around Richard in a way he had never before heard. The sound of the Promise Keepers singing "Holy, Holy, Holy" would remain dear to Richard for the rest of his life.

Richard had always been a loving husband, and a father who cherished his children, but when he came home from Promise Keepers he was "on fire." He had been a Christian since age six, but after the PK conference, Richard was more determined than ever to serve God and to serve his family. Richard wanted to be everything that God wanted him to be. The day he came home, he said to Dottie, "Now I know what it means to be on fire for God!"

Three days later, Richard was diagnosed with a malignant brain tumor.

Dottie vividly recalls the couple's reaction: "We were on our knees before the Lord, asking, 'O, Lord, please take it away!' This couldn't be happening. Not to us! We were a wonderful young Christian family, totally devoted to one another and to the children God had blessed us with. Surely God needed marriages like ours to show others how he meant it to be. He wouldn't split us up!"

Two weeks later, Richard underwent a procedure called radiosurgery. It was an all-day hospital procedure and a frightening affair for the family. Nevertheless, Richard's attitude was upbeat and positive. He had special T-shirts printed with the words BE BOLD, BE STRONG across the front. The slogan was a takeoff on the words of the Old Testament leader Joshua, spoken to the Jewish people as they were about to enter the Promised Land. Friends, family members, and fellow church members who were at the hospital to help support Richard and the family all sported the T-shirts. Even Richard himself wore one into surgery. He wanted everyone at the hospital to know where his faith was centered.

Over the next six weeks, the Byrds lived in Columbus in

order to be close to the hospital, where Richard could receive daily radiation treatments. It was an ordeal, but again, a friend sent Dottie and Richard matching shirts with Scripture slogans, which the couple wore to the hospital every day. No one on the hospital staff who knew Richard and Dottie had any doubts about the couple's faith. During that time, Richard and the family continually listened to Promise Keepers tapes for encouragement and inspiration.

After radiation treatments, Richard was given a three-week reprieve before he was due to begin chemotherapy. In the interim, Richard surprised Dottie with a trip for just the two of them to Marathon, Florida. Dottie remembers, "We basked in the sun—and in each other. We walked, we biked, we canoed, we even parasailed! Mostly, we just enjoyed being together, which was what we did best."

The trip to Marathon was the respite before the real marathon. Dottie and Richard knew that the chemotherapy was going to be difficult. It turned out to be a nightmare. In an attempt to shrink the tumor, Richard received an aggressive experimental protocol—three days of intravenous infusion of two chemo drugs at the same time. As frequently happens, the chemotherapy made Richard deathly sick. On the fourth day of each treatment, he was able to come home, only to be quarantined for two weeks. Each day, Dottie had to give him four shots of a drug to build his immune system. Richard was repeatedly readmitted to the hospital's intensive care unit with pneumonia and other complications, and there received further transfusions.

One doctor told Richard, only half-jokingly, "The chemo is going to kill you before the tumor will have a chance to."

Throughout the ordeal, Richard kept with him those things that he considered most important and precious—a photograph of Dottie and him on their wedding day, their children's pictures, his Bible, and his Promise Keepers tapes. Finally, after four months of treatments, Richard said, "No more!" He went off the chemotherapy completely.

Richard decided that God was in control of his life, and God could heal him, if he chose to do so. At that point, Richard said that the quality of his life was more important to him than the quantity.

Interestingly, the months that followed were wonderful for Dottie and Richard and their children. Says Dottie, "We did not have much money, since our only income was from Richard's disability checks, but God provided for our needs. We took one day at a time and enjoyed each other to the fullest. We knew from the beginning that our course of action was Richard's choice. At any point, if the pain became too great he could change his mind [about receiving the chemo]. It was my choice to stand behind him, whatever he chose. We also reassured each other that God was in control. 'Either way, Richard wins,' we'd say, 'and either way, we will have no regrets.' "

Amazingly, Richard regained his strength. Richard and Dottie viewed the time as a special gift from God. In the spring of 1995, Richard was even able to attend another Promise Keepers conference, this time in Detroit.

Before the tumor had been found, Richard had been an avid jogger, so he began jogging once again. Each year, he had run a five-mile race to benefit the local crisis-pregnancy center. On Labor Day, 1995, Richard, Dottie, Natalie, and Kyle ran the race as a family. Kyle won a prize that day as the youngest of the five hundred contestants in the race, at nine years of age.

Then, in the fall of 1995, Richard's condition began to debilitate. His legs gave out on him unexpectedly, at first only occasionally, but then more frequently. Further tests revealed that the swelling in Richard's brain was increasing. In November, Richard was admitted to the hospital with pneumonia and a blood clot. After a round of antibiotics and blood thinners, the doctors inserted a filter into one of Richard's arteries to catch any further clots. He came home the next day, but had to stay on morphine to endure his fierce headaches. The following morning, Richard fell again, this time lapsing into unconsciousness due to seizures in his brain. Dottie called the ambulance and Richard was once again raced to the hospital. The doctors said there was little left for them to do. The swelling in Richard's head was increasing too rapidly. It was only a matter of time.

The doctors said there was one procedure that could be done, a one-time attempt to relieve some of the pressure, but the medical staff made it clear to Dottie that it could only be performed once. Dottie agreed. On November 19, the doctors performed the procedure, and almost miraculously, Richard responded. He was able to get up and visit with family and friends. He was groggy, but functioning.

Word quickly circulated that Richard was dying. Friends came to the hospital from miles away to see him one last time on earth. Each person who came to visit Richard was greeted with a warm embrace by Richard himself, sometimes accompanied by a joke as well. At one point in the parade of visitors, however, Richard asked everyone except Dottie to leave the room for a few minutes. Then, in the quietness, he leaned over to Dottie, took her hand, and asked, "Why is everybody here? Am I dying?"

Dottie was straightforward. She told him that the swelling had increased, and she reminded him that God was still in control. "We don't know what tomorrow brings, but either way, you win."

Richard answered with a smile, "If this is dying, this isn't bad."

That night, the nurses allowed Dottie to remain in the hospital and lie next to Richard on his bed. The couple spent the night holding hands. On November 20, 1995, Richard Byrd woke up and looked at his wife, and squeezed her hand twice. "I love you," he said to Dottie. And she knew he did.

Then Richard fell into an unconscious state, never again to awaken in this life. Dottie and the children stayed by his side all day long. Friends and loved ones came by to visit, and many stayed with the family. Dottie asked for some Promise Keepers music to be played near Richard's bedside. As the music played, she recalled how excited Richard had been when he first came home from the Indianapolis PK conference. He could hardly stop talking about the breathtaking sound of the sixty-two thousand men singing "Holy, Holy, Holy."

Toward evening, just as the song "Holy, Holy, Holy" began to play near Richard's bed, he breathed his last; and at age thirty-four, Richard Byrd was dead. Or, as Dottie put it, "Richard fell into the arms of Jesus. Richard's death was more peaceful than I could have dreamed possible. I could never have imagined such a beautiful ending!"

The days preceding Richard's funeral were numbing, yet rewarding. Dottie remembers: "Richard's life was to bring glory to God, so shall his death be. I believe God inspired every detail at this point for his glory. We mentioned Richard's commitments as a Promise Keeper in his obituary. It was talked about through his [funeral] service. A friend brought a Promise Keeper lapel pin to be put on his suit to be buried with him. When it was time to choose our memorial stone, under our names, I had them engrave A PROMISE KEPT."

Richard Byrd was quite a man, a man of integrity who lived life to the fullest, who faced the worst that death could deal, but he was not afraid. He kept his promises to God, and he kept his promises to Dottie and to their children. Dottie Byrd is quite a woman, too. Rather than running as far away as she could get from all the memories of her husband's association with Promise Keepers, eight months later Dottie Byrd went to the 1996 Promise Keepers conference at the RCA Dome—as a volunteer worker.

Who are the Promise Keepers? After studying this modern men's movement for several years, I am more convinced than ever that—like it or not—they are who they say they are. They are men who want to develop a deeper relationship with God, men who want to be better husbands and fathers, men who are willing to lay aside their own selfish desires for the benefit of their families and society at large, men who are committed to changing the status quo, and most of all, men who are not ashamed of the Gospel of Jesus Christ.

Toward the middle of 1996, Bill McCartney began quoting one particular Scriptural passage, Acts 5:38–39, to members of the media near the close of many of his press conferences. The speaker in these verses is a man named Gamaliel, a leading member of the Jewish Sanhedrin. Now, barely two months after Jesus' death and resurrection, his disciples were spreading the word everywhere that Jesus Christ had conquered death. For preaching about Jesus, Peter and some of the other followers of Christ were hauled into court before the Sanhedrin. Several members wanted to deal with Christ's disciples the same way they had with Jesus, suggesting that Peter and the others be put to death. At this suggestion, Gamaliel, a wise and honored teacher of the law, stood to speak. He first warned the Sanhedrin to be careful how they dealt with the followers of Christ. Gamaliel reminded his colleagues that many charlatans had arisen in Israel before, and after a while, they usually self-destructed on their own, with little or no help from the religious or civil authorities. Then, concerning the early Christians, Gamaliel uttered one of the most profound bits of wisdom ever recorded: "Leave these men alone! Let them go! For if their purpose or activity is of human origin, it will fail. But if it is from God, you will not be able to stop these men; you will only find yourself fighting against God" (NIV).

This, says Bill McCartney, is the theme of what Promise Keepers is about. "God is doing something," he says. "Don't let it pass you by [because of] previous mistakes or contradictions you have seen."[1] Watch us, McCartney seems to be saying, and if you observe closely enough, you will discover that Promise Keepers is not a human effort; it is a God-thing.

Are the Promise Keepers for real? I believe they are. At times during my work on this project, I became frustrated at what seemed almost paranoia in some of the Promise Keepers' professional staff, especially those whose assignments were to make sure that Promise Keepers presented a spit-shined image to the public. Their attempts to "manage" Bill McCartney and the public perception of PK seemed contradictory to the very openness that makes McCartney and other PK leaders so believable. Yet despite my exasperation with the Promise Keepers hierarchy, and specifically the few "gate keepers" of PK information who seemed to have their own agenda, I found nothing to discredit their sincerity. Nothing that might cause one to disparage their motives.

Furthermore, as I moved among the hoi polloi, the everyday Promise Keepers, I found a marvelous spirit of cooperation and openness, unlike that of any other group I have witnessed. Frankly, it was downright refreshing.

Will this new men's movement last? Hard to tell. It could easily go the way of the Men and Religion Forward Movement, a Christian men's movement founded in Maine nearly one hundred years ago, which enjoyed a short-lived popularity and then disappeared into obscurity. Or it could join the "Iron John" crowd, the stalled 1980s men's movement. Whether the Promise Keepers movement survives, one thing is certain—the sparks they have fanned into flames in some men's lives will continue to burn.

Can Promise Keepers as an organization truly change the fabric of a society? I doubt it. But can individual Promise Keepers—even those who manage to keep only a few of the promises they have made—transform our world for good? I am certain of it.

Is Promise Keepers for you? I encourage you to look into it. What do you have to lose? You needn't fear that, once you get close to PK, you won't be able to escape. You can walk away at any point . . . but my guess is that you won't want to. One thing is sure: You will not encounter Promise Keepers and come away unaffected.

I promise.

NOTES

CHAPTER 1

1. Joseph Shapiro, "Heavenly Promises," *U.S. News & World Report*, October 2, 1995, p. 68.
2. Joe Conason, Alfred Ross, and Lee Cokorinos, "The Promise Keepers Are Coming," *The Nation*, October 7, 1996, p. 12.
3. Speech, World Links Conference, Callaway Resort, Pine Mountain, Georgia, July 14, 1996.

CHAPTER 2

1. Bill McCartney with Dave Diles, *From Ashes to Glory* (Nashville, TN: Thomas Nelson Publishers, 1995), p. 286.
2. Ibid., p. 287.
3. Scott Raab, "Triumph of His Will," *GQ*, January 1996, pp. 129–30.
4. McCartney, *Ashes*, p. 290.
5. Ibid., pp. 290–91.
6. Ibid., p. 291.
7. Ibid.
8. Richard Hoffer and Shelly Smith, "Putting His House in Order," *Sports Illustrated*, vol. 82; no. 2 (January 16, 1995), p. 30.

CHAPTER 3

1. *What Is a Promise Keeper?*, cassette tape (copyright © Promise Keepers, P.O. Box 103001, Denver, CO 80250).
2. *Seven Promises of a Promise Keeper* (Colorado Springs, CO: Focus on the Family Publishing, 1994), p. 9.

3. E. Glenn Wagner, *The Awesome Power of Shared Beliefs* (Dallas, TX: Word Publishing, 1995), pp. 98–99.

CHAPTER 4

1. *Seven Promises*, p. 53.
2. Ibid.
3. "Spiritual, Moral, and Ethical Purity," *Defining Moments*, Promise 3, PK videotape (Boulder, 1994; copyright © 1996, Promise Keepers, P.O. Box 103001, Denver, CO, 80250).
4. *Seven Promises*, p. 94.
5. "Purity," *Defining Moments*, videotape.
6. "Raising the Standard in Our Marriages," *Defining Moments*, Promise 4, PK videotape (Denver, 1995).
7. "A Father's Legacy," *Men of Action*, vol. 5, no. 3 (Summer 1996), pp. 4–5.

CHAPTER 5

1. "What Does America Believe?" *George*, December 1996, pp. 115–16.
2. George Barna, *Virtual America* (Ventura, CA: Regal Books, 1994), p. 46.
3. Ibid.
4. Bill McCartney, Promise Keepers solicitation letter, November 4, 1996, p. 2.
5. "The Atlanta Covenant," as reprinted in *New Man*, June 1996, p. 20.
6. Ibid.
7. Max Lucado, "Denominational Harmony: Leading from Bondage to Freedom," *Defining Moments*, Promise 6, PK videotape (Clergy Conference, Atlanta, 1996).
8. McCartney, *What is a Promise Keeper?*, cassette tape.

CHAPTER 6

1. "The Miracle of Faith," *Men of Action*, vol. 5, no. 2 (Spring 1996); p. 12; quarterly newsletter published by Promise Keepers.

CHAPTER 7

1. Gregg Lewis, *The Power of a Promise Kept* (Colorado Springs, CO: Focus on the Family Publishing, 1995), pp. 177–78.
2. Promise Keepers 1996 "Break Down the Walls" stadium syllabus, p. 4.
3. Bob McDowell, "Team Spirit," *New Castle News*, July 11, 1996, p. 1.

4. Cami Schaubroeck, "Wives Approve of Promise Keepers," letter to the editor, *New Castle News*, July 23, 1996, p. 12.

5. Joseph P. Shapiro, "Heavenly Promises," *U.S. News & World Report*, October 2, 1995, p. 70.

6. Laurie Goodstein, "Christian Men's Movement Prays to a Packed House," *Washington Post*, May 28, 1995, p. A-8.

7. *Seven Promises*, p. 79.

8. Ibid., p. 80.

9. Ibid., pp. 73–74.

10. John M. Swomley, "Promises We *Don't* Want Kept," Watch on the Right (column), *The Humanist*, January/February 1996, p. 35.

11. *Seven Promises*, p. 75.

12. Jeff Wagenheim, "Among the Promise Keepers," *New Age Journal*, March/April 1995, excerpted in the *Utne Reader*, January/February 1996, pp. 76–77.

13. Donna Minkowitz, "In the Name of the Father," *Ms.*, November/December 1995, p. 67.

14. Ibid., p. 68.

15. Ibid., p. 69.

16. Wagenheim, "Among the Promise Keepers," p. 75.

17. "God's Priceless Resources," *The PK Volunteer*, July 1996, p. 4.

18. Holly G. Miller, "Real Men Keep Promises," *Saturday Evening Post*, July/August 1996, p. 84.

CHAPTER 8

1. Bill McCartney, various speeches; but the essence of this material was adapted from McCartney's message at Oakland in 1995: "The Power of a Promise Kept," *Defining Moments*, videotape. Parts of this message are also documented in Janssen, *Seven Promises*, and in Raab, "Triumph of His Will."

2. Ibid.

3. Ibid.

4. Ibid.

5. Ibid.

6. Ibid.

7. Ibid.

8. Wagenheim, "Among the Promise Keepers," p. 75.

9. Press conference, Promise Keepers conference, RCA Dome, Indianapolis, IN, July 27, 1996.

10. Press conference, Promise Keepers conference, Three Rivers Stadium, Pittsburgh, PA, July 13, 1996.

11. J. Sebastian Sinisi, "Keepers Pledge $1 Million to Rebuild Black Churches," *Denver Post*, June 23, 1996, pp. 1A, 6A.

12. Ibid.

13. Interview with the author, July 13, 1996, Pittsburgh, PA.

14. *What Is a Promise Keeper?*, cassette tape.

15. Press conference, Promise Keepers conference, RCA Dome, Indianapolis, Indiana, July 27, 1996.

16. Ibid.

17. Louis Templeman, "Racial Reconciliation: The Possible Dream," *Ministries Today*, November/December 1993, p. 42.

18. Ibid., p. 46.

19. Press conference, July 27, 1996.

20. Ibid.

21. Press conference, July 27, 1996.

22. Press conference, July 27, 1996.

23. Speech, Pittsburgh Promise Keepers Conference, July 13, 1996.

24. Ibid.

25. Ted Olsen, "Racial Reconciliation Emphasis Intensified," *Christianity Today*, January 6, 1997, p. 67.

26. "Promise Keepers Statement on Biblical Reconciliation," Promise Keepers 1996 conference syllabus, pp. 10–11.

27. Press conference, July 27, 1996.

28. E. Glenn Wagner, *The Awesome Power of Shared Beliefs* (Dallas, TX: Word Publishing, 1995), p. 182.

CHAPTER 9

1. Pastor Jack Stephens, "The Seven False Premises of Promise Keepers," *The Ohio Bible Fellowship Visitor*, August 1995, p. 4.

2. Ibid., p. 4.

3. Speech, regional Promise Keepers conference, Portland, OR, October 12, 1991.

4. David W. Cloud, "Beware of Promise Keepers," *O Timothy*, vol. 11, no. 6 (Oak Harbor, WA: Way of Life Literature, 1994), p. 1.

5. Dr. L. K. Landis, "Should Involvement in PK Be a Test of Fellowship Among Independent Baptists?" *The Baptist Challenge* (Little Rock, AR: September 1996), p. 10.

6. "Resolution on Promise Keepers," passed at the Independent Baptist Fellowship of North America Annual Conference, Seattle, WA, June 20–22, 1995.

7. Landis, "Involvement in PK," p. 10.

8. Steve Rabey, "Where Is the Christian Men's Movement Headed?" *Christianity Today*, April 20, 1996, p. 49.

9. Ibid.

10. Ted Olsen, "Racial Reconciliation," January 6, 1996, p. 67.

11. *The Tidings*, March 31, 1996, issue, published by the Roman Catholic Archdiocese of Los Angeles.

12. Rabey, "Where Is the Christian Men's Movement Headed?," p. 60.

13. Ann Rodgers-Melnick, "Promise Keepers Attracts Mainstream Supporters," *Pittsburgh Post-Gazette*, July 11, 1996, p. A-3.

14. Douglas DeCelle, "Among the Promise Keepers: A Pastor's Reflections," *Christian Century*, July 3–10, 1996, p. 696.

15. Ibid., p. 697.
16. Ibid., pp. 696–97.
17. Ibid., p. 697.
18. Lucado, "Denominational Harmony," *Defining Moments*.

CHAPTER 10

1. Nancy Novosad, "God Squad," *The Progressive*, August 1996, p. 26.
2. "Building Men of Integrity," PK brochure, 1996.
3. Suzanne Pharr, "A Match Made in Heaven," *The Progressive*, August 1996, p. 28.
4. Novosad, "God Squad," p. 25.
5. Ibid.
6. Ibid., p. 27.
7. Conason, Ross, and Cokorinos, "The Promise Keepers Are Coming," p. 16.
8. Pharr, "A Match Made in Heaven," p. 29.
9. Wagenheim, "Among the Promise Keepers," p. 76.
10. Charles Colson, "Raising the Standards in the Brotherhood of Believers," *Defining Moments*, Promise 6, PK videotape (Minneapolis, 1995).
11. Rabey, "Where Is the Christian Men's Movement Headed?," p. 60.
12. Speech at Promise Keepers' 1996 Clergy Conference, Atlanta, GA, February 14, 1996.
13. Conason, Ross, and Cokorinos, "The Promise Keepers Are Coming," p. 12.

CHAPTER 11

1. Debbi Wilgoren, "In the Land of Promise," *Washington Post*, May 24, 1996, p. E-1.
2. "International Expansion," *Men of Action*, Summer 1996, p. 13.
3. Ibid.
4. Ibid.
5. Ibid.
6. "Partners from the North," *Men of Action*, Summer 1996, p. 13.
7. Ibid.
8. "International Expansion," *Men of Action*, Summer 1996, p. 13.
9. Bill McCartney, PK solicitation letter, November 4, 1996.

CHAPTER 12

1. Speech, World Links Conference, Callaway Resort, Pine Mountain, Georgia, July 14, 1996.

SUGGESTED READING LIST

Blankenhorn, David. *Fatherless America: Confronting Our Most Urgent Social Problem*. Dallas: Basic Books, 1995.

Bly, Robert. *Iron John*. New York: originally published by Addison-Wesley Publishing Company, 1990; first Vintage Books edition: Random House, 1992.

Cole, Edwin Louis. *On Becoming a Real Man*. Nashville: Thomas Nelson Publishers, 1992.

Dalbey, Gordon. *Healing the Masculine Soul*. Dallas: Word Publishing, 1988.

Keen, Sam. *Fire in the Belly*. New York: Bantam, 1991.

Lewis, Gregg. *The Power of a Promise Kept*. Colorado Springs: Focus on the Family Publishing, 1995.

McCartney, Bill. *From Ashes to Glory*. Nashville: Thomas Nelson Publishing Company, 1995 edition. Originally published in 1990.

Morley, Patrick M. *The Man in the Mirror*. Nashville: Wolgemuth & Hyatt Publishers, Inc. 1989.

Seven Promises of a Promise Keeper. Colorado Springs: Focus on the Family Publishing, 1994.

Trent, John. *Go the Distance*. Colorado Springs: Focus on the Family Publishing, 1996.

Wagner, E. Glenn. *The Awesome Power of Shared Beliefs*. Dallas: Word Publishing, 1995.